ELDERS
REFORMED

ELDERS
REFORMED

TIM BAYLY
JÜRGEN VON HAGEN

Elders Reformed

Warhorn Media
2401 S Endwright Rd.
Bloomington, IN 47403
WarhornMedia.com

Unless otherwise indicated, all Scripture quotations are from the NEW AMERICAN STANDARD BIBLE®, © 1960, 1962, 1963, 1968, 1971, 1972, 1973, 1975, 1977, 1995 by The Lockman Foundation. Used by permission.

Cover design by Ben Crum and Alex McNeilly. Front cover photo by Adrian Infernus on Unsplash. Back cover photo by Dibya Jyoti Ghosh on Unsplash.
Interior layout by Alex McNeilly. Typeset in 11/14 Garamond Premier Pro.

ISBN-13: 978-1-940017-27-3 (paperback)
ISBN-13: 978-1-940017-28-0 (EPUB)
ISBN-13: 978-1-940017-29-7 (Kindle)

To all elders who, as good shepherds,
faithfully love their sheep and carefully guard their flocks,
doing the hard yet excellent work our Lord has called them to;
and specifically,
to Don Jerred and Joel Belz,
for their inspiration to us as pastors

◆

Contents

Acknowledgments

THIS BOOK WOULD NOT HAVE BEEN WRITTEN without the help and support of many individuals. We thank our dear wives, Mary Lee and Ilse, for their patience with us while we worked on this project. We are grateful to our editors at Warhorn Media, Nathan Alberson, Alex McNeilly, and Jacob Mentzel, who did an excellent job reviewing earlier drafts, editing the text, and cutting redundancies; and our designer Ben Crum for his fine work. We thank the elders and pastors at Trinity Reformed Church in Bloomington, Indiana, for their trust and support of our work. We are grateful to the Taylor family for letting us use their residence on Lake Michigan, where this book originated and much of it was written. Most of all, we thank the Lord for His Church and the many good elders He has called to this office whom we have been blessed to work with.

ELDERS
REFORMED

From the care of the ewes with suckling lambs He brought him
To shepherd Jacob His people,
And Israel His inheritance.
So he shepherded them according to the integrity of his heart,
And guided them with his skillful hands.

—Psalm 78:71–72

LIFE
&
DEATH

ELDERS ARE A BLESSING OR A CURSE.

They're never insignificant.

Jesus said, "I am the Good Shepherd." Then He warned His disciples against bad shepherds. He called bad shepherds "hirelings" and told us how to tell the difference.[1]

When the wolf attacks, the good shepherd fights to protect the sheep. He gives his life up for his sheep. The hireling, though, abandons his sheep.

The good shepherd dies so his sheep may live, while the bad shepherd saves his own life and kills his sheep. I was going to write that the hireling allows his sheep to die—not that he kills them—but that wouldn't be true.

Once I[2] was talking about decision-making with a Marine who served

---

1. John 10:11ff.

2. Since we wrote this book together, it is sometimes difficult to use the first-person singular pronoun. We felt that inserting the name of the author it refers to each time would disturb the flow of the text too much. Here is our solution: because Tim Bayly is the one of us with the greater experience of

3

in Vietnam. I told him my dad had frequently warned us that to *not* make a decision *was to make* a decision, and he agreed. He added that the worst thing an officer could do in the military was to avoid making a decision. Then he told a story.

His squad had been assigned a new squad leader and they went out on patrol. Right away, they came under fire.

My friend paused, then continued: "When we came under fire, the guy ran for cover."

"So what happened?" I asked. His running for cover seemed perfectly natural to me.

"That was the *worst* thing he could have done."

"Really? Why?"

"Because his job is to protect his men—not protect himself."

"So then what happened?" I asked.

"When we got back, he was reassigned."

"Did someone report him?"

"Yes."

Not yet seeing the weight of the story, I probed: "Wouldn't it be dangerous to report him? Wouldn't he get angry at the guy that turned him in?"

My friend had been wounded twice during the Battle of Huế. Each time, after his wounds had been attended to, he'd been sent back into the battle.

He was quiet for a second, then softly he said, "He was just happy to be alive."

Being dense, I kept at it: "Why?"

"In 'Nam, lots of times he would have been killed."

"By whom?"

"One of his men. Happened a lot."

We were on a long drive and things went quiet for a while.

Elders are shepherds and they're either good or bad. Never neutral.

That day I didn't learn as much about decision-making as I did about being a pastor, an elder, a shepherd. The shepherd's first concern must be

---

pastoral service, assume the first-person singular refers to him, unless indicated otherwise. We realize this might lead readers to assume the entirety of that section is also by Tim. But, taken as a whole, this work is the product of both of us. In a few cases, we have left the narrator intentionally ambiguous to maintain the anonymity of those involved in the story being told.

protecting his sheep. Marines know it. Pastors and elders should know it even more. Bad shepherds don't just allow their sheep to perish.

They kill them.

Sheep Need Shepherds

During the three years of our Lord's public ministry the Jews had many shepherds. There were Pharisees, Sadducees, priests, scribes, and elders. These men had been called to feed and protect God's sheep, but what was the condition of their flock?

Looking out over God's people, our Lord pitied them. Why? "Because they were distressed and dispirited like sheep without a shepherd."[3]

Sheep without a shepherd are painfully troubled and without hope and guidance. They are pitiful to watch.

Jesus set to work to remedy the situation. First he commanded His disciples to pray: "The harvest is plentiful, but the workers are few. Therefore beseech the Lord of the harvest to send out workers into His harvest."[4]

Jesus told His disciples to pray for more shepherds who would work to protect the sheep God calls His own. Remember the promise our Lord made to Simon Peter and his brother, Andrew, when he called them to leave their fishing nets?

"Follow Me, and I will make you fishers of men."[5]

Pastors and elders are fishermen. We share the work of gathering God's harvest, of calling men[6] back to the kingdom of God and the safety of His righteousness.

Seeing the vulnerability of God's sheep, Jesus told His disciples to pray for more shepherds, and He trained His disciples to be shepherds themselves. The apostles were the first shepherds of the Christian church and much of their work was choosing, preparing, and ordaining other shepherds who would help them carry out this critical work.

---

3. Matthew 9:36.
4. Matthew 9:37–38.
5. Matthew 4:18–19.
6. Because God Himself named our race—men together with women—*adam*, Hebrew for "man" (Genesis 1:26–27), we will honor this usage.

God's people are not made to fend for themselves. We're weak and vulnerable. That's why God calls us "sheep." Sheep need shepherds.

When God brought His people up out of Egypt and they began their journey to the Promised Land, Moses was their shepherd. Caring for them meant a terrible workload, and it was burning him out. Moses' father-in-law, Jethro, saw the problem and counseled Moses to appoint more shepherds.[7]

Moses took his advice and set apart one man in ten. Do the numbers: one in ten is ten in a hundred, a hundred in a thousand, a thousand in ten thousand, ten thousand in a hundred thousand, and a hundred thousand in a million. If the city of Indianapolis were the sons of Israel under Moses, he would have appointed nearly ninety thousand men to help him shepherd God's flock. And this does not even take into account that there were also elders of higher ranks—leaders of fifty, one hundred, and one thousand. There has always been a lot of conflict among God's people and it is wise to have a lot of elders to do the work.

The same priority is seen in the New Testament. The apostles appointed elders in every city and every church:

When they had appointed elders for them in every church, having prayed with fasting, they commended them to the Lord in whom they had believed.[8]

Again:

For this reason I left you in Crete, that you would set in order what remains and appoint elders in every city as I directed you.[9]

Note that in both cases the word is "elders," not "elder." Plural, not singular. We speak of this as "the plurality of the eldership," and it's foundational to Presbyterianism.

"Presbyter" is a transliteration into English of the Greek word *presbyteros*, which means "elder." "Presbyterian" indicates that the church is led and shepherded by a group of men called "presbyters" or "elders."

7. See Exodus 18.
8. Acts 14:23.
9. Titus 1:5.

Speaking personally, I can't count the number of times I have exclaimed to my wife, "I'm so thankful for the plurality of the eldership!" Sure, it sounds sort of stilted, but that's what I say. The older we've gotten, the more precious this principle of government has become to both of us.

We're not ashamed to say we love our elders—not just the men in the churches we currently serve, but all the elders we've ever served beside. They are the church's heroes. They are the men Jesus told His disciples to pray for. They are the men Jesus trained. They are the men the apostles appointed in every church and every city of the New Testament.

What's at Stake

Have you been called and set apart by the laying on of hands and prayer to serve the church as a shepherd? Are you a church planter pleading with God to give you such men to help you? Are you a simple Christian who wishes you had shepherds in your church—shepherds who will work alongside your pastor to care for you and your family? To feed you? To guard and protect you?

Are you a young man who aspires to serve your church as a shepherd? If so, it is a good calling you long for. So says the Apostle Paul: "It is a trustworthy statement: if any man aspires to the office of overseer, it is a fine work he desires to do."[10]

The Apostle Paul here speaks of "overseers," the Greek word being *episkopos*, which is the root of our English word "bishop." But the New Testament uses *presbyteros* and *episkopos* interchangeably. These words refer to the same role of elders in the Early Church. The office of an elder is a fine work. It is beautiful. Excellent. Worthy of aspiration.

God's flock needs shepherds. Without them we are harassed and helpless. Without them we die. And if our shepherds are like the squad leader leading those Marines in Vietnam who was more concerned about his own life than the lives of his men—may God have mercy on us.

This is a book about elders. It's about the duty of elders to feed and protect their sheep. If you are an elder, this book will teach you how to follow the Good Shepherd in giving up your own life for the sheep He

10. 1 Timothy 3:1.

purchased with His own blood. This is your calling. If you're not an elder, this book will help you love and submit to your elders.

Make no mistake: shepherding God's sheep is a matter of life and death. It's no exaggeration to say the work of elders is eternally more important than any squad leader in the Marines. At stake are the immortal souls of men, women, and children.

For shepherds of God's flock, the most sobering passage of Scripture must be the warning given to the elders of the Ephesian church by the Apostle Paul when he was on a layover at the harbor in Miletus:

> Be on guard for yourselves and for all the flock, among which the Holy Spirit has made you overseers, to shepherd the church of God which He purchased with His own blood. I know that after my departure savage wolves will come in among you, not sparing the flock; and from among your own selves men will arise, speaking perverse things, to draw away the disciples after them. Therefore be on the alert.[11]

It's all sobering. "Be on guard." "Savage wolves." "Not sparing the flock." "From among your own selves." "Be on the alert."

Most sobering of all, though, is his statement that the flock they are to shepherd was "purchased with His own blood." Whose blood?

The blood of our Good Shepherd. Shepherds who abandon their calling to guard the sheep betray the blood of the Lamb of God.

---

11. Acts 20:28–31.

The elders who rule well are to be considered worthy of double honor, especially those who work hard at preaching and teaching.

—*1 Timothy 5:17*

THE
ELDER

THIS BOOK HAS FOUR SECTIONS, AND THIS FIRST section begins with the elder himself. What is an elder? Where does the office of elder come from? What are the qualifications for this office?

Eldership is an office of responsibility and authority. We start there.

Early in my ministry when I was serving in the mainline Presbyterian Church (USA), it was a fad to have husbands and wives, both ordained ministers, serving as a congregation's "co-pastors." Sometimes, instead of a husband and wife, it was two male pastors. Often it was an older pastor approaching retirement and a younger pastor people anticipated would be his successor. (I never heard of two women serving as co-pastors, but that may have been done too.)

Whether husband and wife or two unrelated men, co-pastorates rarely ended well. The radical egalitarianism of the French Revolution is a procrustean bed that deforms human institutions and relationships. Jesus didn't blush to declare his submission to His Father while He was among us, nor did the Apostle Paul blush to command the obedience of churches, pastors, and elders.

So again, the office of elder is an office of authority. Don't hide it. Don't deny it. Don't cloud its definitions. Don't give any quarter to men who try to impose radical egalitarianism on the officers of Christ's Church. In the church, as in everywhere else, radical egalitarianism will bear the fruit of hypocrisy and conflict.

Our Egalitarian World

Back when I was serving for a year at First Presbyterian Church in Boulder, Colorado, a well-known radio preacher was invited to come and preach. On Monday morning the pastoral staff had breakfast together at a restaurant and asked questions of our guest.

That particular morning, one question asked was how our friend and his elders made decisions in their session meetings.[1] Did they typically vote on things, or not?

With pride, our guest explained to us that he and all his elders never made a decision until they'd reached consensus, by which he meant unanimity. He said unity was very important to them and they wouldn't proceed until everyone agreed. Being young and naive, we were wowed and expressed the requisite admiration for such a wonderful practice of biblical equality.

Our senior pastor was a man of discretion and wisdom. Also meekness. He waited until the guest left for the airport. We had our private room for a while longer and sat at our tables talking about this and that. Then our senior pastor got our attention and said, "You men understand what he meant by waiting until there was consensus for any decision to be made, don't you? He meant no decision was made until everyone agreed with the senior pastor."

That was all. Our pastor was not being argumentative. He wasn't

---

1. In Presbyterian churches, "session" refers to the elders and pastors who meet together regularly to make decisions. Typically moderated by the senior pastor, some churches in the Reformed tradition call this group the "consistory."

defensive. There was no trace of sarcasm, cynicism, or jealousy. Just a simple statement of fact unveiling an important truth. A word to the wise. Unanimity depends upon radical egalitarianism for its appeal. Often, though, unanimity is simply the result of the minority being intimidated into silence.

Likely none of us ever forgot it. I certainly haven't, and from that day to this I've tried to discipline myself in structures and leadership never to pander to or even pay lip service to egalitarianism.

It is said that, back in the day over in Scotland, pastors and elders were skeptical of session decisions that were unanimous. It's good to remind session members of this so minority opinions aren't squelched. Think how often the majority opinions of the children of Israel were wrong. Think how often the Apostle Paul was the minority opinion in the New Testament church. Think how often fathers have to stand against their entire household, including their beloved wife.

The egalitarianism of Galatians 3:28 is right: "There is neither Jew nor Greek, there is neither slave nor free man, there is neither male nor female; for you are all one in Christ Jesus." As children of God by faith in our Lord Jesus Christ, we are all equal. By contrast, radical egalitarianism, which denies the need for leadership and authority, is wrong. More than wrong, it is evil. Yet it has metastasized across the Western world for centuries now, not sparing churches and their elders boards. God ordains authority and man hides, denies, and defies it to his own destruction.

Co-pastorates don't work. They always yield more—not less—conflict, especially between husband and wife. The mutual submission taught by every seminary professor in the country is wrong. Scripture doesn't teach it and it doesn't work.

Concerning session votes, although it postures itself as protecting the equality of all members of the session by not making a decision until all agree, the rule of consensus doesn't so much promote equality as much as it squelches the minority. Egalitarianism never makes good on its false promises.

Elders under Authority

So why this at the beginning of the book?

Elders who serve the church well, using their authority for the safety, sanctification, and contentment of their sheep, demonstrate submission to authority themselves. This is always the case with any authority. If a woman is seeking wisdom for whom to marry, she should begin by asking herself whether this man she is considering demonstrates submission to authority. In the same way, men and women thinking about joining a church should seek a congregation whose elders submit to one another, and whose elders together submit to their pastor.

Yes, in Christ there is neither Jew nor Greek, slave nor free, male nor female. So in a certain sense there is also neither pastor nor elder; the session is all one in Christ.

But that said, every political institution, business, army, school, household, and church has officers and authority. Even the feminist *Ms.* magazine had a vertical masthead listing publisher, editor in chief, managing editor, and so forth. From high to low, top to bottom, first to last. We may fight all we want against this universal law God has placed across all creation, but leadership and authority are inevitable because God has ordained them. And no church or session that tries to hide or deny its own authority is doing anyone a favor. Leadership and authority are a cornerstone of man's existence and those who fight against it will find themselves crushed by it.

Church Government Is Up for Debate

This is a book about elders, and we know there are many churches that have no officers called elders. There are many variations of church government, and you can make a good case from Scripture for most of them. Some churches have officers called deacons who function much like elders. In chapter 6 of the Book of Acts, deacons are appointed to resolve conflict in the church concerning the distribution of the food given for the help of the widows. Some thought the Hebrew widows were getting more than their fair share, so the church appointed men of good judgment and respected by the members of the Jerusalem church to govern this church charity in such a way that no one felt slighted.

As we look at the office of elder biblically, we'll see from the beginning it's been focused on resolving conflict. In this sense we could say the deacons appointed in the Jerusalem church functioned as elders. We could also say Jerusalem's deacons functioned like pastors, since Stephen was a deacon and his preaching the Word of God led to his having the privilege of becoming the first Christian martyr.[2]

Let's go into this book on elders acknowledging that Scripture does not lay out a cohesive, carefully defined form of government for the Christian church. Reading the New Testament, we note similar responsibilities being carried out by officers bearing different titles, and we see the same title being used for men whose work is quite different. In fact, there are New Testament titles and offices some believe the Holy Spirit no longer calls men to because they were uniquely for the New Testament church and time.

The leaders of the Protestant Reformation thought the office of apostle ceased after the Apostolic Age. This was John Calvin's conviction, but then he spoke of his fellow Reformer Martin Luther as an extraordinary case, referring to him as an "apostle."[3]

Beyond the variety of convictions concerning which individual offices are biblical and should be held by men in the church today, there is the related issue of what overall form of government is biblical.

Three Forms of Church Polity

There are three forms of government commonly practiced in Protestant churches:

- Congregationalism
- Presbyterianism
- Episcopacy

Congregational churches have a congregational vote on all sorts of things from church budgets to church discipline, all the way up to

---

2. See Acts 7.

3. John Calvin, *The Bondage and Liberation of the Will: A Defense of the Orthodox Doctrine of Human Choice against Pighius*, ed. A. N. S. Lane, trans. G. I. Davies, Texts and Studies in Reformation and Post-Reformation Thought (Baker, 1996), 28.

excommunication. They usually have a pastor and often deacons as well. Typically the pastor functions as the spiritual leader with authority over doctrinal matters, whereas the deacons focus more on administrative and financial matters. Often in Congregational polity, churches have both a board of trustees, which focuses more on financial and church-house matters; as well as a board of deacons, which consults with their pastor concerning his spiritual leadership of the flock. Of course there's great variety among Congregational churches, but the main thing is that Congregational government's center of authority is the common assembly of believers in each local church.

Presbyterian churches have fewer congregational votes than Congregational churches, because Presbyterian government's center of authority is the board of elders (usually called the "session"). Presbyterian churches delegate most authority to the elders, who make the majority of the decisions and carry out the discipline of the church's members (including excommunication). Presbyterian polity is analogous to representational democracy in political government.

Another distinction between Congregationalism and Presbyterianism is that Congregationalists have no court of appeal. The decision of each congregation is final.

Most Presbyterian churches have courts of appeal above their local church to which they can appeal the ruling of their elders. One such court is called the "presbytery." This is a group of pastors and elders from a number of churches who meet a few times each year, and one of their main responsibilities is watching over the peace, unity, and purity of its pastors and member churches.

Episcopal churches are led by priests (pastors) who are subject to their bishop, who oversees a number of priests serving a number of churches. Many Episcopal churches have something like a parish council composed of leading members of the church who bear much of the responsibility delegated to elders in Presbyterian churches and deacons in Congregational churches. Such councils make key decisions concerning programs, budgets, and ministries, also consulting with the priest concerning his spiritual leadership of the flock. It is only reasonable that those permanently dwelling in the midst of any church should aid the priest in his preaching and pastoral care of individuals, since council members usually stay in the church for decades, whereas priests and pastors come and go.

But the central authority in Episcopal churches—and particularly the authority to appoint priests to parishes and discipline them—is lodged in the bishop himself.

One of these three forms of government—Congregationalism, Presbyterianism, Episcopacy—is the way most Christian churches are governed. We can say that once we get past the titles given to offices and look carefully at the way churches function, there is a certain inevitability to the plurality of the eldership. Congregational, Presbyterian, and Episcopal churches each follow Scripture in appointing men in every church who live permanently in the midst of the people and bear a significant part of the responsibility and authority for the well-being of the souls in their flock.

Our Commitment to Presbyterianism

What about you and your church? Earlier we warned that the elder is not a pastor. This was not an attempt to get into an argument with readers who view their pastor as the church's elder or whose deacons function much like the elders in a Presbyterian church. Just as good arguments can be made from Scripture for each of the forms of government above, good arguments can be made from Scripture for a variety of church officers called a variety of names, such as overseer, bishop, deacon, and elder.

But since this is a book for elders, and since the Greek word *presbyteros* means "elder," and since it is the Presbyterian form of polity that places the greatest weight and authority on church elders, and since your authors believe that Presbyterian government with a plurality of elders (what Calvin refers to as "an assembly of elders"[4]) most closely matches what we see in Scripture, please understand and accept our writing on the subject as not in any way polemical, but as grounded in those premises. In other words, we hope many will read this book and find helpful ways to apply it to their own churches, even if their church polity is Congregational or Episcopal.

---

4. Comments on 1 Corinthians 5:4, *Commentary on the First Epistle to the Corinthians*, trans. John Pringle, (Books for the Ages, 1998), 151.

Our Commitment to Three Offices

One final note on polity before we move on. Even in churches that are Presbyterian and have a plurality of elders leading and exercising the authority vested in them by the congregation, some of those churches are "two-office" and others "three-office." Which is to say, some Presbyterians believe there are three scriptural offices that should be filled in every church: deacon, elder, and pastor. Other Presbyterians believe there ought to be only two: deacon and elder, but no pastor. The elders who hold to the two-office view say there is no office of pastor in the New Testament, so we ought not to have pastors today. They argue that all authority should be held in the hands of a group of elders with no man above or below any other man.

Iain Murray wrote an article on this debate saying he'd studied the issue and could not argue from Scripture one way or the other; that the Bible can be read to support both the two-office and three-office views.[5]

That said, we have written this book from a three-office view believing this view best represents both the teaching of Scripture and the almost universal practice of the Church across the centuries. We do not condemn the two-office view, yet we believe it's better to take one side and write a book on the eldership from that side, fully acknowledging to our readers that this is our view of what is best.

We defend our commitment in two ways. First, practically. As a matter of fact, those churches and denominations holding to a two-office view almost always practice a distinction between the elders, placing one of them in a position different from the others. Even among two-office churches, it's typical for one elder to lead the elders meetings and do most of the preaching. Sometimes, also, he administers the sacraments of baptism and the Lord's Supper, and it's common for him to carry the heaviest load of pastoral care for the members of the congregation.

Such churches do not refer to their head elder as "pastor," even though he is the elder responsible for moderating the session meetings and congregational meetings, he does most of the pastoral counseling, he is the man who typically officiates over the sacraments of baptism and the Lord's

5. Iain Murray, "Ruling Elders: A Sketch of a Controversy," *Banner of Truth Magazine*, no. 235 (April 1983), 1–9.

Supper, and he does most of the preaching. Regardless of the nomenclature used in your own denomination or congregation, here we will refer to this man as "pastor."

Almost every Presbyterian church has such a man, and it's natural for him to be helped by the elders, while being particularly trusted by the sheep he feeds from the pulpit week in, week out, year after year. The sheep know his voice, and it's natural for them to listen and follow him most closely.

Five centuries ago, Pastor Martin Bucer, who worked closely with John Calvin, pointed out this perfectly natural tendency:

> Even in the apostles' time one of the elders was chosen and ordained as a superior in this office, presiding over all the others and bearing and carrying out to the furthest and highest degree the care of souls . . .
>
> In the same way the rule in the first church at Jerusalem is presented to us: for St Luke describes James as presiding over the whole congregation and all the elders; in the fifteenth chapter of Acts he recounts how in the council of the church after Peter it is James who speaks before all the elders. . . . The same order was also perpetually maintained in other churches, as far as we can tell from the evidence of church history, and also all the most ancient fathers, such as Tertullian, Cyprian, Irenæus, Eusebius, and others. And this is also required by the human need that whenever there are matters in which many people are involved, one or perhaps a few need to be appointed to preside over the others, speaking and acting on their behalf.[6]

We said we'd give two reasons for our commitment to three offices, though, and we end with this Scripture:

> The elders who rule well are to be considered worthy of double honor, especially those who work hard at preaching and teaching.[7]

This verse is anything but a slam-dunk proof that each church is required

6. Martin Bucer, *Concerning the True Care of Souls*, trans. Peter Beale (1538; Banner of Truth, 2009), 37. All quotations from Bucer throughout are taken from this work.

7. 1 Timothy 5:17.

by the Word of God to have deacons, pastors, and elders. Nevertheless, this is our practice.

Summing up then, for the purposes of making this book a coherent whole and teaching what we ourselves have learned serving in our own Presbyterian form of church government, we will speak of three offices—deacon, elder, and pastor—understanding these offices to differ from each other as follows:

- Deacon: an office of mercy and compassion
- Elder: an office of rule and authority
- Pastor: an office of rule and authority with particular focus on teaching and preaching

Once more let us declare that we are firm believers in elders. As pastors, we have learned the wisdom and joy of serving alongside men who share in the work of the ministry with us. To some degree, this book will be an extended argument for the plurality of the eldership. If you give us your minds and hearts, we think it's likely, regardless of your own congregation's polity, that you will become convinced that you should have some men sharing the load of peacemaking, pastoral care, and discipline with your pastor or priest.

If so, God has blessed our work, because this is our goal. We believe in elders. We don't know how we would do our work without elders to share the load with us. We rejoice that God has provided us godly men who do their work as elders without complaint, but joyfully.

May God bless your church with the same.

For this reason I left you in Crete, that you would set in order what remains and appoint elders in every city as I directed you.

—Titus 1:5

CHAPTER I

What Are Elders?

THIS IS A BOOK FOR ELDERS.

But what is an elder?

Literally, an elder is someone older. In Scripture the Greek word translated "elder" is *presbyteros*. Eye doctors diagnose a condition called presbyopia, which Mayo Clinic defines as "the gradual loss of your eyes' ability to focus on nearby objects." They add, "It's a natural, often annoying part of aging."[1]

Myopia is the opposite of presbyopia, and this eye condition is commonly diagnosed in childhood and adolescence. If you have myopia, you have no problem seeing objects close to you, but objects further away are blurry.

Why all this business about eyes? Well, there's no single piece of God's creation that doesn't teach us His truth. Old people naturally start to focus less on what's right in front of them, and more on what's some distance away

---

1. Mayo Clinic, s.v. "presbyopia," accessed February 23, 2019, https://www.mayoclinic.org /diseases-conditions/presbyopia/symptoms-causes/syc-20363328.

from them. Elders see things in the distance more accurately. Thus they are gifted for making better decisions for the church's protection and peace.

Tribes, states, nations, families, clans, and churches all appoint elders to lead them. What these elders are called differs by tradition. In our form of government here in the United States we call them "president," "justice," and "senator." In state and local government they are titled "governor," "mayor," "judge," "supervisor," and "councilman." Tribes are led by a "chief" who in turn leads the "tribal council."

At this point, we can hear some protests.

Because older people have better eyesight for the distance doesn't necessarily mean their wisdom about the future is any better.

True enough, but are we really going to deny that age and wisdom walk hand in hand? Isn't wisdom largely the fruit of accumulated experience? Don't we see this in the athlete's reps? The musician's practice? The pilot's flight time? The anniversaries celebrated by the husband and wife? Isn't this the meaning of references to "the school of hard knocks," that in any job, as our mistakes pile up, we learn from them and get better?

Sure, but some people never learn from their mistakes. We shouldn't just assume older people are wiser. Some older people are fools and some younger people are wise beyond their years.

True, but the old phrase "the wisdom of age" is an old phrase because it's generally true. In fact, old sayings themselves are generally old because they're generally true. The fact that there's not a one-for-one correlation between age and wisdom is no reason not to go to older men and women for wisdom. Old age is no guarantee for wisdom, but young people are less likely to have it. Start to look for wisdom by looking for someone older than yourself, but before you choose one individual, weed out the old fools.

But what if we look for an older person and we find all the older people around us are cynical or corrupt? What if we find they haven't gained wisdom over the years, but rather have become skilled in extorting sexual favors and taking bribes?

Yes, this happens with some regularity in the life of man, and we must be on guard against allowing corrupt old men and women to fool us, robbing us of our virtue and hope. In such cases, remove the elders from their office and get younger ones who are wise "beyond their years." Churches sometimes are best served by younger elders, and those older members who object may be objecting precisely because they have not aged well and resent those younger than themselves who *are* aging well.

In other words, in the church "elder" is a placeholder not so much for age as for wisdom, faith, and godliness. Much better to call into the eldership a young man whose character lines up with the elder qualifications listed in many places of the New Testament than to call an older man who is a drunk, or who is greedy, or who is led by his wife.

Elders Are Shepherds

Back at the time of the Reformation, Pastor Martin Bucer said this about the importance of elders (whose office he includes as he speaks of "the pastoral office"):

> Because so much is involved in the pastoral office, with teaching, exhortation, warning and discipline, comfort and pardon; and for this a reputation, a sense of awe, and an example of life are required; and since the whole of this so varied ministry has to be carried out in such a way as to help any and every one of the elect; every Christian can easily see how various kinds of exalted gifts and skills are needed, as well as all the earnest zeal, for the proper execution of the pastoral office. . . .
>
> . . . And since the Lord has also bestowed and distributed the gifts necessary for this office not to one or two, but in different ways to many, it was his will that his churches, if they were able to have meetings and essential order, should have elders, whether few or many, according to the requirement of each congregation.[2]

Scripture affirms that sheep must have shepherds, and within Presbyterian polity we believe the pastor should share leadership and authority with several elders. One benefit of this form of government is that elders

2. Bucer, 33, 34–35. The full title in the original was *Concerning the True Soul-care and the correct shepherd-service, how the same should be established and executed in the church of Christ.*

tend to be permanent members of the community, whereas pastors come and go. This means the elders are often more trusted than the pastor. In the exercise of authority, particularly in various forms of church discipline, the elders uniquely represent the people and are trusted by them.

Presbyterian polity prevents the pastor from being high-handed in his leadership. Exhortations, admonitions, rebukes, and excommunications given and applied by the people's trusted representatives have more of a chance of being accepted by the congregation as a whole, and thus we make a principle out of this plurality of the eldership meaning not one, but several (and sometimes a bunch of) elders.

Years ago in a used bookstore I came across an old book of worship forms and liturgies put together by a Princeton Seminary theology professor named Archibald Alexander Hodge. Looking through it I came across a service plan for the ordination and installation of elders which, since then, I have used in all our services for the ordination and installation of elders. The first paragraph reads,

In the first planting of the Christian Church the apostles went about ordaining several Elders in every city. A distinction is affirmed by Paul between those Elders who as ministers of the gospel labor in word and doctrine, and those Elders who only rule. These Ruling Elders are in a special sense the representatives of the people, chosen by them for the purpose of exercising government and discipline in conjunction with pastors or ministers of the word. It is proper that the government of the Church should be in the hands of several men of wisdom and piety, rather than in the hands of one, and especially that the pastor should be counseled and assisted by persons of reputation living permanently in the midst of the people, in perfect sympathy with them and enjoying their confidence. Thus in the Presbyterian Church have the people secured control of their own church affairs, and prevented the growth of professional clerical bigotry and tyranny.[3]

3. Archibald Alexander Hodge, ch. 6, "Order for the Ordination of Elders," *Manual of Forms for Baptism, Admission to the Communion, Administration of the Lord's Supper, Marriage and Funerals, Ordination of Elders and Deacons, etc. Conformed to the Doctrine and Discipline of the Presbyterian Church* (Presbyterian Board of Publication, 1882), 51–52.

Sadly, through the years many churches have been led by pastors who do not fear God. Instead of loving and protecting His flock, they flatter their rich members and consolidate their power over the congregation while doing little or nothing to oppose false doctrine and immorality. Restoring the biblical dignity and calling of elders would go a long way to preventing such clerical tyranny.

The church today needs more elders who are committed to pastoral care. We need more shepherds who give up their money, reputation, and lives for their sheep. This book is our attempt to honor this calling. Our Lord Himself said He was the Good Shepherd, and it's a great privilege for these church officers to imitate Him in this work.

We must restore the work of shepherds in Christ's Church. The apostles appointed elders in every church. The Scriptures provide many verses laying out the qualifications and duties of such men. Sometimes these men are called "overseers," sometimes "elders," sometimes "bishops," but what they hold in common is their duty to shepherd the sheep:

> I exhort the elders [*presbyterous*] among you, as your fellow elder [*sympresbyteros*] and witness of the sufferings of Christ, and a partaker also of the glory that is to be revealed, shepherd the flock of God among you, exercising oversight not under compulsion, but voluntarily, according to the will of God; and not for sordid gain, but with eagerness; nor yet as lording it over those allotted to your charge, but proving to be examples to the flock. And when the Chief Shepherd appears, you will receive the unfading crown of glory.[4]

Bad Elders

Now then, before we bring this chapter to an end, we must acknowledge how often elders, church boards, and parish councils themselves go bad. Pastors can go bad, but so can elders.

We will warn against the temptations and sins that corrupt the work of elders while also teaching what Scripture declares this work and calling to

4. 1 Peter 5:1–4.

be. We've already named a couple temptations and sins of pastors. What are a some sins typical of elders?

Two of the most common are, first, elders who view themselves as the pastor's loyal opposition, protecting the congregation from his zeal and faith; and second, elders who despise their pastor, considering him a lazy man who works one day a week and couldn't survive or support his family out in the "real world."

Both sins in time bear the fruit of power struggles that divide the elders board, and often the church as well. Bad elders are typically men who have spent their lives commanding everything and everyone around them, and who have come to view the congregation as their own personal fiefdom with pastors representing a threat to their control. Jürgen remembers an elder once accusing him: "You have wrested our church out of our hands!"

Was it ever "his" church?

It can be easy to think this or that pastor is the problem until the church's history is read in the elders' minutes or elicited from elderly members during home visits. Then it becomes clear such an elder is as divisive among the elders and within the congregation as he is with the pastor, and souls are strewn across the path he has walked unhindered through his years sitting in his catbird seat as ruling elder.

It will be a foundational principle in this book that the mark of the good shepherd is that he fights the wolves and lays his life on the line to protect his sheep. He never runs from the wolf.

Bad pastors and bad elders must both be kept from the sheepfold. Failing that, they must be thrown out. Otherwise the wolves will eat the sheep. Then, as Hebrews 13:17 warns, the shepherds will have to give an account to the Chief Shepherd for the death and destruction that occurred under their watch—for the loss of the souls they were called to guard and protect.

There's a beautiful note of grace between God the Father and His only begotten Son shortly before our Lord went to the cross. It's found in what we refer to as Jesus' "High Priestly Prayer." Jesus is about to die and depart, so He pleads with His Father to unite and protect His disciples. But in transferring the work to His Father, note the report Jesus gives of His own work:

While I was with them, I was keeping them in Your name which You have given Me; and I guarded them and not one of them perished but the son of perdition, so that the Scripture would be fulfilled.

But now I come to You; and these things I speak in the world so that they may have My joy made full in themselves. I have given them Your word; and the world has hated them, because they are not of the world, even as I am not of the world. I do not ask You to take them out of the world, but to keep them from the evil one.[5]

Did you note our Lord's words?

"I was keeping them in Your name."

"I guarded them and not one perished."

If you are an elder, you have been called to keep the sheep and lambs in Jesus' name, guarding and protecting them from the evil one. Jesus did the same work. He was faithful and gave an accounting to His Father for each of His sheep.

One day soon you will give the Chief Shepherd an accounting for each of your sheep. Will you be found faithful?

---

5. John 17:12–15.

Moses' father-in-law said to him, "The thing that you are doing is not good. You will surely wear out, both yourself and these people who are with you, for the task is too heavy for you; you cannot do it alone. Now listen to me: I will give you counsel, and God be with you.

—Exodus 18:17–19

CHAPTER 2

Where Do Elders Come From?

FROM THE TIME OF THE NEW TESTAMENT, Christian churches have been ruled by elders. But eldership did not originate in the Christian church. As a form of government, it goes back much further. We find its origins in the people of Israel, God's people.

Old Testament Eldership

Before the family and descendants of Abraham went to Egypt to escape the famine in the land of Canaan, they were ruled by the patriarchs Abraham, Isaac, and Jacob. Patriarchy means government by the father, the head of the household and highest authority of the family. The father decided where the household lived and what it did to make a living. He determined the rules of the family. He allotted family property to the members and judged between them in times of conflict.

Patriarchy is derived from the rule of God the Father, "from whom all fatherhood in heaven and on earth derives its name."[1] His fatherhood is

---

1. Ephesians 3:14.

expressed in His statutes and commandments, His blessings on all who keep them and His retributions to all who break them, and His loving care for His people.[2] God calls Israel His firstborn son, and Himself Israel's Father.[3]

Sometime after the descendants of Abraham had moved to the land of Goshen in Egypt and had grown to be a people, they adopted their form of government by elders, most likely copying it from the Egyptians. That the Egyptians had elders in positions of leadership is suggested by Genesis 50:7, which speaks of the "elders of [Pharaoh's] household and all the elders of the land of Egypt."

We find the first mention of elders of Israel in the Bible in Exodus where God, speaking to Moses from the burning bush, told him to "go and gather the elders of Israel together" and tell them that their God is moved by their suffering in Egypt. Moses was told to take the elders and go with them to Pharaoh, king of Egypt, and demand permission to go and sacrifice to their God.[4] The people were too numerous to come together and consult with Moses so they were represented by elders.

When the Israelites had left Egypt and were wandering through the wilderness to meet their God at Mount Sinai, Moses' father-in-law, Jethro, came to visit him. Seeing that Moses was overwhelmed by the work of judging the people, hearing and settling disputes and solving conflicts, Jethro advised him to appoint able men to help him in a hierarchical structure with leaders of thousands, hundreds, fifties, and tens. These men would settle small disputes so that only the hard and difficult cases would be brought before Moses. Deuteronomy calls these men "leaders" or "heads" and "judges."[5] Thus, from the very beginning, eldership is an office of leadership and of judging conflicts.

The Hebrew word for leader, "head," indicates that the elders go before the people entrusted to them in the same way that Middle Eastern shepherds go before their flocks (instead of walking behind them as Western shepherds do). Moses was to hear and judge only the hard cases, and he was

---

2. See Psalms 68:5; 89:26; 103:13.

3. See Exodus 4:22; Jeremiah 31:9; see also Deuteronomy 32:6, Isaiah 63:16; 64:8, Jeremiah 3:19; Malachi 2:10.

4. See Exodus 3:16–18.

5. Deuteronomy 1:15–16.

the people's representative before the Lord. He commanded the elders to be impartial and without fear of men in their duties as judges. They were to hear all parties involved in a case regardless of status and wealth, for "the judgment is God's."[6] As judges, the elders represented the people and pronounced God's verdict.

The books of Exodus, Leviticus, Numbers, and Deuteronomy give us some indication of the role of elders in Israel. They were instructed by Moses in the Word of the Lord and in their tasks.[7] A select number of them accompanied Moses on the way to the top of the holy mountain.[8] Elders were commanded to lay their hands on the head of the bull of the sin offering, thus discharging the sin of the people on it.[9]

In times of severe conflict, God Himself spoke to a select number of elders and placed on them the Spirit that was on Moses to strengthen their faithfulness and support for Moses.[10] Thus, the office of elder went beyond just civil and judicial administration. Elders had authority in the religious ceremonies, as well as in communication between the Lord and His people.

Deuteronomy 21, 22, and 25 explain how the elders were involved in legal procedures, finding out the truth and passing judgment. Deuteronomy 21 deals with the case of a son rebelling against his parents. The elders hear the case and judge it. The judgment on the rebellious son is binding on the whole community and executed by them.[11] Deuteronomy 22 deals with the case of a man who accuses his new wife of not coming into marriage as a virgin. The elders hear the case, review the evidence, and judge it. Again, their judgment is binding on the community and carried out by it. Deuteronomy 25 deals with the case of a man not performing his family duty to the wife of his deceased brother. The elders hear both sides and give the man a chance to repent. If he does not, they shame him before the whole community.

The general principle here is that the elders represent the whole community as they hear and judge cases of moral misconduct or offenses, and

6. Deuteronomy 1:17.
7. Exodus 18:20; 19:7.
8. Exodus 24:1, 9.
9. Leviticus 4:15.
10. Numbers 11:16, 25.
11. Deuteronomy 21:18–21.

thus their judgment is binding on the entire community. This illuminates what Jesus said about dealing with the offenses of an unrepentant brother. Jesus instructs his disciples first to go to that brother and explain his sin to him. Then, if this brother refuses to listen, they are to take two or three witnesses and state the case in their presence. Then, if he still does not hear, they are to "tell it to the church."[12]

Does that mean we're supposed to reveal the whole sin to the entire congregation? Staunch Congregationalists might say yes, but the tradition and practice of eldership documented above which Jesus knew suggests no. The elders should hear and judge the case on behalf of the congregation, and precisely because they represent the congregation, their judgment is binding and executed by the whole church.

After the people of Israel had settled in the land of Canaan, we find elders at the national level,[13] and at the levels of tribes,[14] clans,[15] and cities.[16] It was the elders of Israel who came to Samuel to demand a king.[17] Later, the elders of Israel made a covenant with David and anointed him king of Israel.[18] In these instances, the elders acted as representatives of the people. We also find them as advisors to the kings of Israel.[19]

The books of Jeremiah and Ezekiel tell us that Israel had elders during the time of the Babylonian Exile, and the book of Ezra shows that eldership again prevailed after the Israelites had returned from the exile.[20] This is confirmed by the apocryphal books of Susanna and First and Second Maccabees, which were written during the post-exilic period. When the Jewish synagogues developed as meeting places for the local Jewish communities in Palestine and in the diaspora sometime during the third century BC, they were headed by elders.

The Gospels and the Book of the Acts mention rulers of the synagogue, men who were responsible for the order of worship in the synagogues and

12. See Matthew 18:15–20.
13. "The elders of Israel." See for example, Joshua 7:6; 1 Samuel 4:3.
14. See 2 Samuel 19:11; 2 Kings 23:1.
15. See Judges 11:5.
16. See 1 Samuel 11:3.
17. 1 Samuel 8:3.
18. 2 Samuel 5:3.
19. See for example, 1 Kings 8:1; 12:6.
20. See Jeremiah 29:1; Ezekiel 8:1; 14:1; 20:1; Ezra 5:5; 6:7; 10:8, 14.

for their administration and were appointed by the elders governing the synagogue. Their Hebrew title "head" suggests that they were elders. At the time of Jesus, the highest Jewish authority was the Sanhedrin, the supreme council which consisted of seventy-one elders. The Gospels almost always mention the elders together with the "chief priests," showing that the civil and religious leadership of the Jews were intimately connected. Together, the elders and the chief priests played a critical role in the killing of our Lord Jesus on the cross.

New Testament Eldership

The New Testament does not tell us how the office of the elder was first instituted in the churches. Its existence is simply assumed and this indicates that the early churches adopted it from the Jewish synagogues. We first encounter elders in Acts 11:30, where the elders of the Jerusalem church are mentioned as the recipients of the financial gift the Christians of Antioch sent there. Acts 14:23 tells us that Paul and Barnabas appointed elders in all the new churches. Later, Paul instructed his young co-worker Titus to appoint elders in every city of Crete.[21]

By always using "elders" in the plural, these and many other passages also indicate that all churches had a plurality of elders. Acts 15 shows that elders, together with the apostles, formed the Council of Jerusalem which judged the question whether non-Jewish Christians had to submit themselves to the Law of Moses before becoming disciples of Jesus Christ.

When the Apostle Paul returned to Jerusalem years later with a financial gift from the churches in Greece, he again met with the apostles and the elders to give an account of his missionary work and to deliver the gift.[22]

The *Didache*, a document likely from the early second century, instructs the churches to appoint elders and deacons, mentioning that they "also serve as prophets and teachers." For several centuries, the *Didache* was a valued book of instruction for Christians and their churches.

Calvin, in his review of the history of the Early Church, writes that in the Early Church there was a distinction between elders who taught and

---

21. Titus 1:5.
22. See Acts 21:17ff.

administered pastoral care to the flock and elders whose task was to exercise church discipline. All churches elected bishops, meaning "overseers," from among the elders. The role of the bishop was initially to lead the assembly of elders and solve conflicts among them. Initially, the status of bishops was essentially the same as the status of elders. However, in the course of time, bishops became increasingly elevated over the elders, and eventually, the office of the elder disappeared altogether.[23]

It returned through the sixteenth-century Reformers of the Church, Martin Luther, Huldrych Zwingli, Martin Bucer, and John Calvin. Subsequently, most Protestant churches adopted government by elders, although the role of elders varies in different denominations and remains strongest in Reformed and Presbyterian churches.

Choosing and Appointing Elders

When eldership was instituted by Moses during the time of the march through the wilderness, he told the people to "choose wise and discerning and experienced men from your tribes, and I will appoint them as your heads."[24] Three aspects of this are noteworthy. First, the future elders were chosen by the people. Second, Moses made them leaders. And third, the men chosen for eldership had to have certain qualifications. All three aspects were later adopted by the Church and remain valid today. In this chapter we deal with the first two. We discuss the qualifications for eldership in chapter 3.

Chosen by the People

Elders are chosen by the people, the members of the local church, to assure that those who will lead and judge them know them and trust them. If they are to represent the community, they should come from its midst and know their people. The work of elders is often difficult and burdensome, especially when they are involved in solving conflict, judging offenses, and caring for the souls of their sheep in difficult times. To do this work boldly and faithfully, elders must know that they have the trust of the congregation.

---

23. See John Calvin, *Institutes of the Christian Religion*, ed. John T. McNeill, trans. Ford Lewis Battles (Westminster John Knox Press, 1960), 4.4–5.

24. Deuteronomy 1:13.

We read in Acts 14:23 that Paul and Barnabas appointed elders in all churches, and in Titus 1:5 that Paul instructed Titus to ordain elders in all cities of Crete. Does that mean that Paul, Barnabas, and Titus personally chose the men they appointed and that those men perhaps did not even come from the local churches? We do not have any information about the exact procedures Paul, Barnabas, and Titus followed, but we do know that what they did was firmly tied to the tradition of the Jewish synagogues.

It is more than likely, therefore, that the men appointed as elders of the churches were chosen from among the flocks. Calvin explains that the Greek word translated as "appointed" in Acts 14:23 implies that there was a vote the congregation took by lifting their hands and suggests that Paul and Barnabas presented two men to the congregation which then decided by vote which one was elected.[25]

This then sounds like a democratic election. It is not. Elders must not run for office like politicians. In a democracy, the elected members of the council or parliament are to represent the interests of their constituencies. In the church, though, it is the Lord of the Church, Jesus Christ, whose approval we seek. Where elders regard themselves as representatives of some groups within the church, the elders will be dysfunctional. One of our elders once said, "I represent those members who pay all the bills." Needless to say, money was the one thing by which he judged every activity of that church. His role on the elders board was constantly destructive until he finally stepped down and left the church. He had never understood the nature of his office as an elder.

So, why then should the congregation vote on the elders? In Acts 20:28, Paul tells the elders of the church in Ephesus that they were made elders by the Holy Spirit. The Holy Spirit had put them into that position.

How did the Holy Spirit do that?

By working through the church, putting into the heart of the members His choice of men for eldership. Calvin writes in his commentary on Acts 13:2,

No election of pastors is legitimate except one in which God plays the leading part. For although He has commanded that pastors and bishops

25. *Institutes* 4.3.15.

be elected by the Church, He has not, for that reason, permitted so much licence to men that He Himself does not preside as the chief Moderator.[26]

While he recognizes the special situation of Acts 13:2 when men were appointed as missionaries of the church of Antioch, Calvin applies the same principle to the office of pastors and elders. The implication is that the church must make room for the Holy Spirit to act within it, showing which men to elect. That is, the election of elders must be prepared by times of prayer.

Every church member should pray for good elders and for the Holy Spirit to show him or her who that is in their church. The church as a body should pray before the election, asking the Holy Spirit to reveal His will. Another implication is that the sitting elders should always be observing their flock to see whether there are men who might in the future qualify for this office.

How so? Calvin writes in the same place, "There is no need that the Spirit should cry to us out of heaven, that he whose election is in question is divinely called."[27] Instead, he explains, the congregation, by observing the men and the gifts God has given them, can recognize who has been called by God to be an elder and who has not. This, of course, implies that only men who are well known and recognized by the congregation should be elected as elders, and that all members make efforts to get to know them.

In order to assure that only men are appointed as elders of whom the church as a body has been convinced by the Holy Spirit that they are the right ones, many churches have rules requiring a supermajority for a person to be elected—some two-thirds, some three-quarters, and some even more. This also assures that the elected elders know the congregation trusts them.

Elders should be elected by the congregation, but this alone is not enough. Calvin calls the vote of the congregation the "external" call to the office and emphasizes that the external call must come with an "internal

26. Calvin, *The Acts of the Apostles 1–13*, trans. John W. Fraser and W. G. J. McDonald, vol. 6 of *Calvin's Commentaries*, ed. David W. Torrance and Thomas F. Torrance (Eerdmans, 1965), 352.

27. Calvin, *Commentary on the Acts of the Apostles*, trans. Christopher Fetherstone, ed. Henry Beveridge (Books for the Ages, 1998), 411, 853n784.

call," that is, a man's sincere conviction that he qualifies for the office and desires it. As Calvin put it, the internal call is "the good witness of our heart that we receive the proffered office not with ambition or avarice, not with any other selfish desire, but with a sincere fear of God and desire to build up the church."[28] He goes on to note that this is not just a matter of feeling and desire. A good shepherd needs to have knowledge of the Word of God and of the church he desires to serve, as well as maturity and wisdom.

The Bible assures us that God equips those He calls into any service in the church with the necessary gifts,[29] which means that asking whether one has the gifts to be a good shepherd is part of verifying one's call to office. A man must pray to recognize and confirm that internal call, but it is wise to also ask one's wife, friends, and Christian brothers for their judgment. Sometimes, a man who later turns out to be a good elder needs a suggestion from someone else to start contemplating the possibility.

Appointed by Leaders

Moses told the Israelites to choose men from among themselves whom he would then appoint as their heads. Note that the election by the congregation was not sufficient for them to be leaders. They needed to be put into that position by Moses, and, in doing so, Moses gave his consent to the people's choice. It is clear then that Moses had authority over the elders of Israel.

Acts 14:23 suggests something similar. We noted above that the appointment of elders by Paul and Barnabas certainly involved a vote by the congregations. But, at the same time, the word "appointed" indicates again that Paul and Barnabas had a position of authority in the process. Calvin suggests that they acted as moderators of the congregational meeting where the election took place to assure that no conflict nor disorder would arise that might lead to the election of a person unfit for the office and he recommends that, therefore, "other pastors ought to preside over the election in order that the multitude may not go wrong either through fickleness, through evil intentions, or through disorder."[30]

28. *Institutes* 4.3.11.
29. See 1 Corinthians 12:4ff.; Romans 12:3ff.; 1 Peter 4:10–11.
30. *Institutes* 4.3.15.

Calvin's interpretation of Titus 1:5 is similar: Titus was to preside over the church meetings in which elders were elected, making sure that the process was done in an orderly and appropriate fashion. This was then confirmed by the laying of hands on the men appointed as elders by Paul, Barnabas, Titus, or Timothy.

That the role of these men presiding over the elections was not merely assuring due process is clear from the Apostle Paul's admonition to Timothy to "not lay hands upon anyone too hastily and thereby share responsibility for the sins of others."[31] Paul here speaks of elders and their ordination and warns Timothy not to ordain men prematurely, which is to say, before they have proven their maturity in the faith and their qualification for the office. It is clear, then, that the pastors presiding over the election have a responsibility in assuring that no one is appointed an elder whose qualifications they are not convinced of.

Churches today can and do have a variety of ways to do this. One of our churches appoints a nomination committee of sitting elders and chaired by the senior pastor. The committee receives suggestions of possible candidates from the members of the congregation. The committee then examines the qualifications of those who have been suggested by at least ten percent of the congregation and presents the candidates the committee deems qualified for the office to the congregation. The congregation then has some time to talk to the candidates. In the end, the congregation votes by secret ballot.

In another church, the elders board functions as the nomination committee, receives suggestions from the members of the congregation, examines potential candidates, and develops a list of candidates which is then presented to the congregation to be voted on. There is no single best way for all churches to do this; much of it depends on the size and the unity of the church. It is wise for all churches, however, to fix the rules of the procedure and make them known to the congregation well ahead of time before the appointment process begins.

Knowing that our hearts "are deceitful above all things"[32] and that we might be tempted to strive for an office for wrong reasons, and knowing that the church may err in her judgment of individual candidates, it would

31. 1 Timothy 5:22.
32. Jeremiah 17:9 (NIV).

be unwise to appoint elders who desire the office without the consent of the church *or* to appoint elders upon a vote by the congregation alone, and equally unwise not to give the (senior) pastor a position of authority in the process. We trust that the Holy Spirit works to call those men into office that our Lord has chosen through the interplay of the roles of the people, the candidates, and the sitting elders and pastors.

You shall select out of all the people able men who fear God, men of truth, those who hate dishonest gain; and you shall place these over them . . .

—Exodus 18:21

CHAPTER 3

What Are the Qualifications for Elders?

A MAN MUST HAVE CERTAIN QUALIFICATIONS to be an elder of the Church. Both Old and New Testaments give us instruction regarding these qualifications.

The Old Testament's Qualifications for Elders

As we saw in the previous chapter, the account of Jethro's advice to Moses in Exodus 18 provides very wise guidance about the work of elders. That passage teaches us not just how these men should be chosen and appointed, but also what such men should be like.

Fear of God

Jethro advised Moses to look for men who "fear God, men of truth, those who hate dishonest gain." These qualifications seem obvious. Since God is Lord over His people, and all men who lead work under and are accountable to Him, nobody should be a leader of God's people unless he fears God.

Matthew Henry comments on this verse: "The fear of God is that principle which will best fortify a man against all temptations to injustice."[1] Leaders must be men of truth, men who are honest and have integrity. They must not take bribes nor seek to enrich themselves at the cost of the congregation. These are questions of character.

Knowledge and Practice of God's Law

Jethro also advised Moses to "teach them the statutes and the laws, and make known to them the way in which they are to walk and the work they are to do."[2] Elders must know the statutes and laws God has given for His people. They must have good, solid knowledge of the Bible.

But that is not all. They must be told "the way in which they are to walk"—that is, a way of living that is appropriate for elders of the Church. In the church, they must conduct themselves in a way that is appropriate to their office. Much of this depends on the time, place, and culture where the church lives, but there are, as we will see shortly, a number of general principles.

Experience

Finally, elders must be taught how to do their work. Jethro did not assume the future elders of Israel would know everything they needed to know in order to be good elders. Moses should teach them. This is a great encouragement. Churches should train men to be elders, yes. But also, men should not be shy nor too proud to receive such training.

Reviewing the experience later, Moses said to the Israelites that he had instructed them to choose "wise and discerning and experienced men" as their elders.[3] In this list, "wise" is a general term which includes "discernment" and "experience." We might read: "wise, that is, discerning and experienced, men." The wisdom of an elder is the ability to know what to do or say in difficult situations, particularly those of uncertainty and conflict.

Remember the story of Solomon who, as a young man, asked God for

---

1. Matthew Henry, comments on Exodus 18:21, *Matthew Henry's Commentary on the Whole Bible* (Hendrickson, 2008), 96.
2. Exodus 18:20.
3. Deuteronomy 1:13.

"an understanding heart to judge [His] people to discern between good and evil"?

God responded to him, saying, "I have given you a wise and discerning heart."[4] Immediately after that, the Bible illustrates Solomon's great wisdom by his judgment in the case of two harlots coming to him fighting over which of them was the true mother of a little baby boy. Since, as we said earlier, the office of an elder is one of judging conflicts, the wisdom it requires is primarily the ability to make good judgments. Elders must have the ability to distinguish between good and evil. Usually, this is the result of life experience and, as Hebrews 5:14 tells us, the constant practice of living under the Word of God.

Inexperienced men—men unable to distinguish between good and evil—should not be elders because they are prone to make bad judgments. Bad judgments undermine the authority of elders and their ability to lead the flock. Bad judgments stir up discontent and conflict in a church. And ultimately, such judgments lead to the church's destruction.

The New Testament's Qualifications for Elders

Building on these principles of eldership in the people of Israel, the Apostle Paul set out the qualifications for eldership in his letters to his younger co-workers Timothy and Titus. Consider 1 Timothy 3:2–7:

> An overseer, then, must be above reproach, the husband of one wife, temperate, prudent, respectable, hospitable, able to teach, not addicted to wine or pugnacious, but gentle, peaceable, free from the love of money. He must be one who manages his own household well, keeping his children under control with all dignity (but if a man does not know how to manage his own household, how will he take care of the church of God?), and not a new convert, so that he will not become conceited and fall into the condemnation incurred by the devil. And he must have a good reputation with those outside the church, so that he will not fall into reproach and the snare of the devil.

4. 1 Kings 3:9, 12.

Paul's list in Titus 1:5–9 is somewhat shorter:

Appoint elders in every city as I directed you, namely, if any man is above reproach, the husband of one wife, having children who believe, not accused of dissipation or rebellion. For the overseer must be above reproach as God's steward, not self-willed, not quick-tempered, not addicted to wine, not pugnacious, not fond of sordid gain, but hospitable, loving what is good, sensible, just, devout, self-controlled, holding fast the faithful word which is in accordance with the teaching, so that he will be able both to exhort in sound doctrine and to refute those who contradict.

Remember that the New Testament makes no distinction between "overseer" (sometimes translated "bishop") and "elder." These are the qualities that make a man fit for the office of an elder. It is unwise to read these passages superficially and treat them like a shopping list, mechanically going through point by point. Much better to first consider the substance and then go through the details.

Blamelessness

Calvin writes, "Only those are to be chosen who are of sound doctrine and of holy life, not notorious in any fault which might both deprive them of authority and disgrace the ministry."[5] Overall, these are qualities of a man's character and his familiarity with and practice of the teaching of the Word of God.

Furthermore, Calvin notes in his commentary on 1 Timothy 3:1–2 that the Apostle takes the excellence (which is his translation of the Greek adjective *kalos* in v. 1) of the office of elder as the reason why a candidate for it must have the qualities he lists: "On account of the dignity of the office, he concludes that it is requisite that he be a man endowed with rare gifts, and not any person taken out of the crowd."[6]

Similarly, in Titus 1:7, the Apostle Paul says an elder must be above

5. *Institutes* 4.3.12.
6. Calvin, *Commentary on the First Epistle to Timothy*, trans. William Pringle (Books for the Ages, 1998), 60.

reproach because he is God's steward. At the time, a steward managed the affairs of a household in the name of the head of the house, so it was an office of considerable authority and responsibility. Again, it is the quality of the office that requires high qualities of the man filling it.

In both instances, Paul begins by saying that an elder must be "above reproach" or "blameless." We might be scared by that requirement, thinking that "blameless" means free of any sin or vice. But, as Calvin points out, if that were what the Apostle had in mind, no man would ever qualify for the office.[7] What is meant, then, is that an elder must not be accusable of some blatant sin or vice, one that is clearly visible and that he does not have under control, because that would undermine his authority as a leader.

Fidelity

In both texts the Apostle Paul puts "the husband of one wife" immediately after saying that an elder must be above reproach. It is obvious this is an important aspect of blamelessness. In view of the sanctity of the relationship between husband and wife which Paul in Ephesians 5 takes as an image of the union between Christ and His Church, the prominence of this requirement is hardly surprising. Paul is not saying a man must be married to qualify as an elder. Rather, if he is married, he must not have more than one wife.

The Jews of Paul's time, and certainly the Greeks and Romans, had a very low view of marriage.[8] As the Early Church father Cyprian explains, Jews were allowed to be married to more than one wife at the same time, and for this reason the Apostle Paul emphasizes an elder must not have more than one wife.[9]

Naturally, this also requires fidelity in marriage since "marriage is to be held in honor among all; . . . for fornicators and adulterers God will judge."[10] A man who maintains sexual relationships outside his marriage is

7. Calvin, comments on Titus 1:6, *The Second Epistle of Paul the Apostle to the Corinthians and the Epistles to Timothy, Titus and Philemon,* trans. T. A. Smail, vol. 10 of *Calvin's Commentaries,* ed. Torrance and Torrance (Eerdmans, 1964), 358.

8. See Matthew 19:1–7.

9. Cyprian, "Homily 10 on First Timothy," accessed on June 16, 2020, http://www.newadvent.org/fathers/230610.htm.

10. Hebrews 13:4.

not qualified for the office. The same applies to an unmarried man; he must not be sexually immoral. Note that the Greek word translated "fornicators," *pornous*, shares its origin with our word "pornography." The man enslaved to pornography is barred from the office of elder.

What about a man who has divorced his former wife and remarried?

There are a variety of opinions on this question. Much depends on the circumstances of the divorce. Was the divorce before the man's regeneration? Did he divorce his wife as an unbeliever? Has the man shown the ability to faithfully stay in a stable marriage afterwards over the course of many years? Wise and sincere judgment by the pastors and elders of a church are required in such cases.

We can group the remaining qualities Paul requires from a potential elder in three categories: character, leadership, and a good reputation outside the church.

Character

The character traits of an elder are that he should be sober, prudent, patient, loving what is good, sensible, just, devout, self-controlled. The character traits not compatible with the office are being addicted to wine, pugnacious, quick-tempered, fond of sordid gain, self-willed, or loving money. Rather than go through the list in detail and state the obvious, let us point out that the character traits required are all among what Paul calls the fruit of the Holy Spirit in Galatians 5:22–23. The incompatible character traits are all among the characteristics of a sinful human nature untransformed by the Holy Spirit as Paul enumerates in Galatians 5:19–21.

Thus we can say that, when we examine a man's qualifications for the office of elder, we are looking for signs that he lives a life guided by the Holy Spirit, rather than the life of an unrepentant sinner. What counts is the big picture, the overall impression of his life. We are not to look for perfection in every single characteristic Paul mentions, since it would be impossible to find a man who has no weaknesses. But a man who takes a position of authority and leadership among the people of God ought to show clear and visible signs of his own sanctification by the Holy Spirit. In this, he must be a role model for the people entrusted to him. How else would he lead and admonish them on their own path of sanctification?

Leadership

The second category is that an elder should have visible leadership gifts. Paul indicates that the first place where we should look for those is in the way a man leads his own family. Look at a man's children and how they behave, and you will see how well he leads. Unruly children and children who are known in public to be troublemakers are an indication that a man's leadership is weak, and he should not be put in a position of authority in the church.

As before, this is certainly a matter of circumstances and demands wise judgment on the part of pastors and elders considering a man as a potential elder. We do not want Christian children who have learned to behave like puppets. Such children may not prevent their father from becoming an elder, but if they are simply focused on conformity and superficial standards, they will never grow into spiritual maturity. Nor do we want Christian children to be undisciplined, not the least because God declares that the discipline of children is a sign of the father's love. If a man does not love his own children, how can he love his brothers and sisters and their children in the church?

Titus 1:6 requires an elder to have, as the New American Standard Bible renders it, "children who believe." Others, including the Revised Standard Version and the English Standard Version, have translated the Greek phrase here, *tekna pista*, as "children" who "are believers." But the word *pista* (from *pistos*) has other meanings as well.

We reject interpreting this phrase as "children who are believers" for two reasons. On the one hand, by implicitly holding a man responsible for his children's lack of faith in Jesus Christ, this interpretation suggests the faith of a man's children is his own doing. But faith is "the gift of God," and no one comes to Christ "unless the Father . . . draws him."[11] We must not deny the sovereignty of God in this. And requiring elders' children to have saving faith may very well promote a culture of hypocrisy.

Thus we agree with the King James Version in its proper translation of this phrase as "faithful children," which would mean that a man's children

---

11. Ephesians 2:8; John 6:44.

are to be obedient. Paul's addition, "not accused of dissipation or rebellion," indicates this is indeed what he had in mind.

As leaders, elders must be vigilant, which is to say, they must be on guard against any harm that might be done to their sheep both from the inside and the outside. This is in line with Paul's command to the Ephesian elders: "Be on guard for yourselves and for all the flock."[12] He warned them particularly of destructive and divisive men who would come from among themselves—that is, their own group of elders.

Good leaders recognize problems and dangers, acting against them long before anybody else sees them. They know that the longer they wait to do something, the greater the problem will be in the end and the harder it will be to address it. This is especially true with regard to destructive developments within the church, because they are often mixed up with personal relationships.

Ability to teach is the third leadership quality required of an elder. Note that teaching is not the same as preaching. Not every elder must have the ability to preach the Word of God.

Still, there are many other forms and modes of teaching in a church—leading small groups, teaching Sunday school or youth groups, instructing new believers about the foundations of the Christian faith, holding a class for young parents on how to raise godly children. Some teaching requires eloquence, other teaching does not. Some teachers speak mostly about principles, others mostly tell stories.

Yes, teaching is hard. But what a man cannot teach he does not really understand. Earlier we saw that wisdom has always been part of the qualifications of elders. Being able to pass this wisdom on is a sure sign of a man having wisdom.

Hospitality is the fourth leadership quality mentioned in these passages. Being hospitable to the members of the church, keeping an open house where they can come in, talk, confess sins, seek advice, and share joys, is a sure sign of love. A man who does not like the company of the people entrusted to him does not love them, and lack of love makes arrogant leaders who lord it over their sheep.

12. Acts 20:28.

Reputation

The third category of remaining qualifications is that an elder should have a good standing with outsiders. Paul demands a good reputation with those outside the church. This may seem surprising. Are not the outsiders enemies of our Lord Jesus Christ? Do they not mock Him and His Church? Why should elders care about a good reputation among them?

The answer is that reputation relates to behavior. That outsiders hold the Gospel in contempt is something Christians cannot change. But they should be careful that their behavior does not add to the contempt, giving outsiders even more reason to mock and slander the church. Of course, that does not mean the church tries to please outsiders by joining them in their sins, nor that the church should soften her teaching against those sins. But the elders in particular should not bring a bad reputation on the church by behaving in ways outsiders find scandalous. If they do, Paul points out, accusations from those outside may become a snare of the devil.

Maturity

The final requirement for elders is that they must not be new converts, and this puts a time dimension on this discussion that offers great relief. What Paul has in view is that a new convert who is not yet mature in his own faith may become either proud, or even desperate if the office of elder is too demanding for him. Maturity is required. But maturity only comes with time, persistence, and exercise.

If you desire to be an elder but find the biblical requirements too demanding for you at this time, you need not despair. God will give you opportunities to grow in your faith and develop what is lacking today. If He calls you, He will equip you with what you need. In time.

Furthermore, remember that you will not be alone in your office as elder. The plurality of elders means you will be in it together with other men. The beauty of it is that your weaknesses will be covered and compensated for by the strengths of your fellow elders, just as your strengths will serve to cover and compensate for their weaknesses. Remember how God gave Moses, a self-confessed leader of slow speech, his brother Aaron to speak for him?[13] You do not have to be the all-perfect elder. Love your fellow elders and you will discover that, together, you can be the group of good shepherds your church needs.

Moses taught the elders of Israel God's laws, and he made known to them how they were to live and work. Jesus spent three years teaching His disciples who would become the future leaders of His Church.

Churches today have an obligation to train future elders, and elders need to be teachable.

---

13. See Exodus 4:10–14.

He said to him the third time, "Simon, son of John, do you love me?"
Peter was grieved because he said to him the third time, "Do you love me?" and he said to him, "Lord, you know everything; you know that I love you."
Jesus said to him, "Feed my sheep."

—John 21:17 (ESV)

PART 2

THE
ELDER'S
WORK

NOW WE TURN TO THE ELDER'S WORK, AND THIS IS the heart of this book. As an elder, you have specific responsibilities assigned to you by God. You have taken ordination vows, and one day soon God will require you to give an account of your faithfulness to His precious flock and sheep—your faithfulness to Christ's Bride.

First, we'll open up some critical aspects of our present cultural context, warning about how much more difficult it makes the work of the elders. Elders today are particularly vulnerable and need the goodwill of their congregation.

We'll follow that with a chapter on ways elders can win their congregation's trust.

Next, we'll talk a bit about conflict, since that (as we'll see) is so much of the elder's work.

Then we will look at the duty of elders to protect the flock as a whole.

There are times when the elders' primary concern must not be the individual sheep, but the well-being of the entire flock—the entire congregation. Groups have a personality. Keeping watch over the congregation is as important as keeping watch over families and individuals.

After that we'll focus on what it looks like to guard individual sheep. Never trust a man who claims love for mankind but never seems to find it in himself to love and care for and sacrifice himself for one particular person. Caring for individual sheep is the center of pastoral care. How is it to be done? How do elders go about seeking the lost sheep? How do we guard each soul? Each marriage? Each household?

Finally, we'll finish this section by addressing the critical work of church discipline.

Then Miriam and Aaron spoke against Moses because of the Cushite woman whom he had married (for he had married a Cushite woman); and they said, "Has the LORD indeed spoken only through Moses? Has He not spoken through us as well?" And the LORD heard it. (Now the man Moses was very humble, more than any man who was on the face of the earth.)

—Numbers 12:1–3

CHAPTER 4

Elders Under Attack

BEFORE WE MOVE ON TO CHAPTERS GIVING some practical help toward building the trust of congregations for their elders, it's important to spend some time opening up our present cultural context. Elders and pastors (as well as fathers) should understand that church officers are increasingly vulnerable to attacks aimed at alienating our congregation's trust, respect, and love for us.

Hatred for Authority

We live in a culture increasingly hostile to everything Christian, and this hostility is most intense in its attack on that male authority which God the Father Almighty decreed from the beginning when He made them male and female, creating Adam first, then Eve.

God is no mother. He is the Father from whom all fatherhood in heaven and earth gets its name,[1] and if we are to serve wisely as elders of Christ's

1. At times, Scripture speaks of God being *like* a mother (e.g., Isaiah 49:14–15; 66:13; Matthew 23:37), but the Bible never says God *is* a mother. Rather He *is* the Father Almighty, Maker of

Church, we must particularly note how He has delegated His authority to husbands, fathers, and elders. This is not to say father-rule is limited to the Christian home and church. Father-authority is God's decree across all creation,[2] but this is a book on eldership, and protecting and building up the authority of elders is our concern.

To do their work, elders must have the trust of their flock, yet today church members are assaulted from all sides by those encouraging them to distrust and rebel against the men God has placed in authority over them. Satan doesn't want our mothers, sisters, sons and daughters, or wives protected by fathers and elders any more than he wanted Eve protected by Adam. He's a snake and his method is always deception in service of rebellion against God.

Because of our culture's hatred for authority, Christian men in positions of authority are quite vulnerable. Wise fathers, for example, are aware that their little ones are often enticed to rebel against them. It's the same with pastors and elders: we do our work well aware that we live on a knife-edge of judgment by those eager to pounce on the slightest exercise of authority, particularly authority exercised by a man. Nowhere is this fomenting of rebellion against male authority more visible than throughout the social media which consume the lives of our loved ones.

Naturally, then, pastors and elders have taken to hiding our authority. Male authority is scandalous in our world, so we downplay it.

Hiding Authority

In many churches today, the Lord's Supper is no longer served by the elders. Instead, elders are augmented and replaced by women and children distributing the bread and wine.[3] For two millennia the authority of male church officers over the sacraments was most visible when those officers distributed the elements of the Lord's Supper, but now no more.

---

heaven and earth, and all fatherhood has its origin in Him, the "Father (*patēr*), from whom all fatherhood (*patria*) in heaven and on earth derives its name" (Ephesians 3:14–15).

2. Note that God commands Noah to bring into the ark two of every species of animal, both "a male and his female" (Genesis 7:1–2). Note also God's punishment of His people in Isaiah 3:12: "Their oppressors are children, and women rule over them."

3. Yes, my wife and I have been served the elements by a minor child in another congregation.

A little story. Around thirty years ago, I was talking to a close friend who told me what had happened the previous weekend with his father. His dad had been visiting his son-in-law and daughter for the weekend and went to church with them. Just prior to the call to worship, the pastor walked to the back of the church where my friend's dad was seated and quietly warned him that he was not permitted to join the congregation in partaking of the Lord's Supper.

Readers are wondering why the pastor did such a thing? We're sorry we are not free to explain it more, but I will tell you how greatly strengthened I was hearing of this a few days later and thousands of miles away—done by a pastor I had never met. From concern for this lost sheep and his family and the name of Christ and the well-being of the flock, this shepherd ran the risk of incurring the wrath of the father, his son-in-law, his daughter, other family members not present, and others in the congregation who noticed or heard of it.

Whether or not they understood his defense or appreciated it, this faithful shepherd defended the sheep of his flock.

Understand this is what is now being hidden by women and children serving the elements. The Church of Jesus Christ is turning away from church fathers who have the responsibility to guard the Body of Christ from scandal through their presiding over this sacred meal. We hide this now by pushing women and children forward visibly—not male elders. But these women and children are not officeholders who have been delegated God's authority for the protection of the Body of Christ.

Similarly, many churches now appoint women to attend their elders meetings. This is sold as an attempt to compensate for the purported inability of men to understand or take into consideration the values and perspectives of women and children. If there is still some minimal, residual adherence to male church authority, appearances are kept up by the female participants not being ordained or installed. (And of course, the session is careful not to allow the women to vote if the vote is an act of formal church discipline.)

As we pointed out above, this kind of thinking is poisonous because elders must never be thought of (or think of themselves) as representatives of this or that constituency. If they do, division is the sure consequence.

Having taken the half-step and recognizing the hypocrisy of church officers asking women to work alongside them without getting the position, ordination, or dignity of an elder has led, in turn, to these women being ordained and installed as elders proper.[4] You know, equal pay for equal work. Increasingly, then, women serve on the elders board as representatives of other women (and children, we suppose). On a number of levels, this is schismatic.

The increasing hiddenness of male authority in the Church is quite evident today. Who would deny that this seems a wise move in our context of relentless attacks on the male authority of husbands, fathers, elders, and pastors?

Women now comprise the majority of seminary students, with even the most conservative seminaries accepting women into their Master of Divinity programs—programs specifically created for and historically serving men preparing for pastoral ministry. In the local church, women teach mixed-sex Sunday school and midweek Bible classes. Women lead their own husbands, children, and other families in home fellowship groups. Women are ordained and installed as deacons, governing the church's distribution of charity to the needy. Women are appointed as lead deacons over male deacons.

Authority is on life support—particularly male authority. Trouble is, in our feminist age, the conventional wisdom is that men should not defend male authority because doing so is self-defeating. The conceit is that, obviously, men are only defending male authority because we have high views of our own sex, low views of the opposite sex, and strong views on protecting all of our male perquisites.

Knowing people would accuse us of being sexist, it's hard for us to resist caring more about our own reputations than about the honor of our heavenly Father and the well-being of His flock. Sadly, then, we have recoiled from the battle and refused to defend male authority. So now we are left

4. Lest the reader think the authors have no experience with such things, a few years prior to my call to my first parish back in 1983, a sixteen-year-old girl had been elected, ordained, and installed as an elder of that church. The congregation had wanted the women and youth of the church to have a representative on the session. Off at college by my arrival, this young woman continued as an inactive elder of our congregation my first years there.

watching women expose pastors who are greedy and sexual predators on social media. From the sidelines, we cluck our tongues in disapproval of such awful male authorities (desperately hoping our own churches and pastors won't be these women's next victims).

It should be obvious, but pastors and elders don't seem to realize that our obsequiousness toward these (overwhelmingly) female whistleblowers is accelerating rebellion against male authority. The cost of pastors and elders fawning over female bloggers' viral posts taking down male authorities is the attenuation of those pastors' and elders' own authority. After all, who was it who failed to discipline these predators back when they were abusing the boys and girls in their churches?

We have met the enemy, and it is us. When male authorities were demanding more fame and fortune for their work and sexually abusing young people, the blame for it all now falls on those male authorities who refused to discipline the abusers. The abuse was there for the male authorities to know about and see, but what did we do to oppose and expose it?

Usually, nothing.

So, with our tails between our legs, we quietly admit that, unless these gutsy women authorities had stepped up, everything would still be hidden. Which leads all of us to thank God for women who do the dirty work of . . .

Disciplining men.

The subtext of our public spectacles of shaming male predators and those male authorities who connived at their sin is promotion of The Big Lie that male leadership is evil.

The Solution

What is the solution?

Certainly not for us to jump on the bandwagon of female empowerment, turning more authority over to women and demanding to be able to sit safe at home while they do combat with God's enemies.

Surveying the attenuation of male authority around and among us, pastors and elders must give ourselves to the hard work of rebuilding our congregations' trust, respect, and love for those men God has called to feed and protect His flock.

Some years back, the elders of a Presbyterian church with a vacant pulpit asked for my help investigating and disciplining incest that had been
discovered in one of their families. It was a complicated case given the large
size of the family, as well as the great span of ages of the abused and abusing
children. My wife Mary Lee and I had some knowledge of the congregation
and were willing to help, so with the permission of our session, we went.

It took a week of work there at the church to finish the investigation;
warn the other members and families in the congregation of the sin among
them and of their own children's vulnerability; institute proper pastoral
care to the parents and children of the specific family; and, of course, report
the crimes to the proper civil authorities.

During the course of the week, each child was interviewed to find out
what he or she had suffered from and/or committed against his or her sib-
lings. Not yet knowing the extent of the father and mother's involvement or
complicity in the incest, both parents had been sidelined in the investigative
process, so neither the father nor mother were present for the interviews.

It came time to interview an eight-year-old daughter of the family. She
was about to go into a room with Mary Lee and three elders' wives when it
occurred to me to speak to Mary Lee and the elders' wives, saying I would
accompany them in this interview.

They were surprised. Why would I insert myself in this particular interview, given that it was with a young girl?

Truthfully, at first it was sort of an incipient sense deep in my gut. I tried
to explain that I had a sense this little girl needed to see some man working
to protect her, and I was the only one available to do it.

We went into the room and sat down with this sweet little girl. Mary
Lee and the elders' wives spoke reassuring words to the girl and began
probing whether she had been involved physically in inappropriate ways
with anyone, particularly her sisters and brothers who had already confessed
their incest to us?[5]

She seemed at ease as she responded negatively to the women's questions. No, she had not been touched inappropriately nor had she touched
anyone else inappropriately. Yes, she knew what her "private parts" were,

---

5. In this case, it was a daughter who initiated and led the incest.

and no one had touched her there. Yes, she understood what we were trying to get at and there was nothing to say.

It had gone on for maybe fifteen minutes. Sitting there listening, I had a growing sense there were things not being said and if I remained silent those things would not come into the open. It was the protection and healing of this little girl we all desired, but it seemed like she was stonewalling the women and the meeting would come to an end if I didn't speak up.

Asking the women if they'd mind if I asked some questions, I turned to the little girl and asked if she understood how serious the sin was in her home and whether she understood how important it was that she tell us what she knew? Then, having brought a man's authority to bear on the situation—and thereby, I thought, a sense of safety—I went back through the questions and asked them again.

It should be no surprise that when a male pastor was the one asking the questions, the answers changed, and we soon learned this little one had also been abused by her older sisters. There was no show of force, no browbeating, no intimidation; and certainly, the gentle questioning was nothing close to what some refer to as "toxic masculinity." Rather, the man who was a pastor questioned this little girl and got an entirely different response than the kind, gentle, women had been getting.

That day something was clarified for me that I'd never consciously known before. If we want trust for fathers, husbands, elders, and pastors to be restored in the Church (at least), we must have fathers, husbands, elders, and pastors show up for the difficult work. Then the Lord will use our work to restore our wives', children's, and church members' trust for us.

At this point some may argue that, generally speaking, women are more capable of helping children—particularly young girls—to divulge the facts and circumstances of their abuse.

But keep in mind this little girl had been abused by sisters. Even if most forensic work with children is done by women, should the church not strive to reestablish the trust of little children and girls for male authority? Is this not a worthy biblical goal for us in our work?

Should we not desire and work toward children trusting their father? Their older brothers? Should we not desire and work toward members of our congregations trusting their pastors and elders to protect them from liars and false shepherds, as well as uncles and choir directors who abuse them sexually? If we cede the dirty work to women, do we not run the risk of contributing to the disrespect, rebellion, and abandonment of male authority?

Learn from this that God has delegated the office and authority of elder to men, not women. Further, it is those male elders who are accountable to Christ for how well they guard and protect His sheep and lambs.

Yes, sure; women also do the work of protection, and rightly so—particularly with the church's lambs. The first alerts will often come from women, particularly pastors' and elders' wives. We are all grateful for their conscientious help and advice in this heavy duty we are to fulfill.

However, some matters are serious enough, with so much at stake and such danger if the work is obstructed or fails, that we learn why God calls men to that work. In the end, there was a need in that room for a male officer of Christ's Church to show himself standing against the sexual depredations committed against this little girl. It was necessary. It was right. It was good. It was what helped this precious little girl to be vulnerable and admit she had been sexually abused.

God has ordained men to serve the Church as the pastors and elders who guard His sheep and lambs. Thus we must not listen or give in to all the pressures we feel seeking to shove us into the backseat in this work.

Now then, let's consider steps we can take to build the flock's trust, respect, and love for their shepherds.

◆

Therefore, I exhort the elders among you, as your fellow elder and witness of the sufferings of Christ, and a partaker also of the glory that is to be revealed, shepherd the flock of God among you, exercising oversight not under compulsion, but voluntarily, according to the will of God; and not for sordid gain, but with eagerness; nor yet as lording it over those allotted to your charge, but proving to be examples to the flock.

—1 Peter 5:1–3

CHAPTER 5

Winning the Congregation's Trust

LOOKING AT THE PARTICULAR DIFFICULTIES we face today as Christian men bearing responsibility for others, we can see the increasing importance of developing tender, loving relationships characterized by trust. This is true for fathers. It's equally true for elders and pastors with their congregations.

What steps can be taken to develop that trust?

Congregational Consent for Elders

The first step is not obvious, but needed. Before ordaining and installing any elder, ask for the congregation to vote on its approval or disapproval of the man. Painful as it can be at times, take a vote on each man. The people ought to trust their elders, and there's no better way of ascertaining trust for a man than asking those he's to lead if they approve him serving as one of their shepherds.

It's long been a principle of Presbyterian polity that no man is ordained to the pastorate without a call from a congregation desiring his work among them. A man may think he has the gifting to be a pastor, but without others agreeing with that gift and formally requesting his service (commonly through presenting him a written "call"), that man's sense of his own gifting and even the pursuit of training and awarding of a Master of Divinity is insufficient reason for him to be ordained.

Presbyterians require such a man to receive a formal call from a congregation wanting him as their pastor before the pastors and elders of the presbytery will act on his ordination.

This requirement of a written call may seem nitpicky, but in his book on pastoral care, John Calvin's fellow pastor and dear friend in Strasbourg, Martin Bucer, declares the importance of the consent of the governed. Bucer includes a section titled "The Choosing and Appointment of Ministers," which points out the biblical necessity of pastors being "reliable men" who have been "well-tested."[1] Then Bucer speaks of the Church's "ancient" practice, writing that the "candidate was not to be ordained to the holy ministry before he had been found blameless by dint of this confirmation and the consensus of the whole church."[2] This resonates with the Apostle Paul's advice to his co-worker, Timothy, that he was not to "lay hands upon [that is, ordain] anyone too hastily," because doing so would make him "share responsibility for the sins of others."[3]

Bucer goes on to point out how Augustine followed this practice by recommending Eradius to the assembled congregation to succeed him as Bishop, seeking their approval of his recommendation. Augustine called Eradius into the church and awaited the people's response. They then approved Augustine's choice by repeated statements of acclamation, ending with seven repetitions of "You are our father, you are our bishop."[4]

The same principle applies to elders. The people should choose their elders, and during their elders' ordination and installation the people should promise to honor and obey them just as they promise to honor and obey their pastor. Yes, the pastor and elders should train and examine the men they present to the congregation for election or confirmation as elders, but

1. See 2 Timothy 2:2; 1 Timothy 3:10.
2. Bucer, 62–63.
3. 1 Timothy 5:22.
4. Bucer, 64–65.

the vote of the congregation should never be bypassed. The present elders should humbly submit their decision to the flock they lead for their approval or disapproval. The flock must be given the occasion to second-guess the pastor and elders' decisions. This is foundational to congregational trust for the eldership.

Outside the church, we understand how important the "consent of the governed" is for harmonious civil order. The English treasure their Magna Carta, and here in the United States we treasure our Declaration of Independence. Consent of the governed is latent in the first and manifest in the second, but both look to the Church who blazed the path before them.

Concerning both the civil and church realms, many arguments have been made that the people are too easily deceived, too subservient to their lusts and passions, and too ignorant to be entrusted with the privilege of gainsaying their enlightened superiors who lead them. Such arguments have always been used by the educated, rich, and powerful to squelch any movement to transfer responsibility and authority to new leadership.

Political leaders can be desperate in their grasp for power, and in this they merely copy religious leaders. Both our Lord and His Apostle Paul were persecuted by civil and religious authorities who perceived them as a threat to their money and political power.[5] Not a few churches today are led by elders entrenched in their authority and both jealous and zealous not to allow any fellow officer—nor even the congregation—to pose any threat to them.

A small clique of elders can control a church for decades. And not at all benevolently, but motivated by pride, self-seeking, and the love of power. Such elders may refuse to allow the congregation any substantive vote on anything. With a show of sadness, they will explain to members who make inquiries that they have not been able to find anyone qualified and willing to serve alongside them on the elders board. Often it's true, but not that other men aren't qualified. Rather, it's true that qualified men are unwilling to serve, given what they know of the pride, self-seeking, and love of power evidenced by these elders who have been in control of the church for the past ten or twenty years.

5. See Matthew 23:1–7; John 7:31–32; 11:47–50; etc.

It's common for such sinful elders, or even one sinful elder, to obstruct attempts by fellow elders, the pastor, or the congregation to add additional elders to the board. If their church's bylaws don't contain term limits for officers, this situation can continue for several generations.[6]

Back, then, to the elders: if we want elders to be trusted by the congregation, we must not bypass the congregation in selecting elders, and sinful elders must not be allowed to become a self-perpetuating power bloc. So, we recommend that congregational votes of approval and term limits for elders be written into each church constitution.

Congregations Moving to Elder Rule

There has been significant growth in the number of churches led by elders recently. Not just in churches with one elder called "pastor," but churches with a plurality of elders who work alongside the pastor. Many churches have changed their bylaws to reflect a growing conviction that the New Testament practice of appointing multiple elders in every city should be restored in our churches today.

As was the practice among the Jews across their history, so the New Testament church believed and practiced a plurality in the eldership. Multiple elders were appointed in each city's church, which is the foundational principle of Presbyterian polity (government).

Again, the three main views of church government practiced across church history are Congregationalism, Presbyterianism, and Episcopacy. We pointed out above that even Congregational and Episcopal churches have bodies that are akin to boards of elders. Almost all those recently moving to Presbyterian polity now were formerly Congregational. However, not many have turned from Episcopal to Presbyterian polity.

We mention this in order to point out that many reading this book will be new to Presbyterian polity and in need of help understanding how it

6. Speaking of term limits, may we make a recommendation? Right now, before there is trouble, amend your bylaws to limit elders and deacons to one three-year term, at which point they must be voted on again by the congregation to a second three-year term. Then, following the second three-year term, require each elder to take a one-year sabbatical before he can serve again. There are many wise reasons behind this common practice. Much conflict has been avoided by this discipline of polity, and we advise your church to consider it.

should and shouldn't work. Start with this truth: those who have moved to Presbyterian government should not assume their newly elected elders will necessarily have the privilege of the congregation's trust and respect.

So then, be careful. It may be tempting for newly elected elders in a formerly Congregational church to want to flex their muscles. "We're elder led now, and that means we elders are to lead" is the shorthand version of what we've observed and are concerned about in such congregations. Inexperienced elders must beware of alienating their congregation at the very beginning simply because they aren't aware they need to build a relationship of trust with them.

Following the institution of Presbyterian polity, it is wise for the session to present the congregation with key decisions, asking them to vote their elders' recommendations up or down.

Yes, it seems counterintuitive. If the congregation has decided to hand over authority to a board of elders, why not trust that the congregation knew what they were doing? Why not go ahead and make the decisions in the session? If the elders have been chosen by the congregation and they think the decision is wise, why ask the congregation to approve it?

One way to answer that question is by thinking about wedding ceremonies, the honeymoon, and the marriages that follow. Yes, the bride has vowed to "obey" her husband, but "many's the slip twixt the cup and the lip." Just because a bride has publicly promised to be subject to the Word of God by being subject to her husband doesn't mean the husband can ride roughshod over his wife, governing their marriage and home by fiat. Wise husbands know (or quickly learn) that there is much hard work in leading a wife, and one of the most important things to learn is that he must work to build his wife's trust in his decision-making. Key to that process is asking for her input on crucial decisions; he must explain the path he'd like to take and why, then asking her what she thinks.

The principle is the same with congregations.

Historically, Presbyterian government has placed a very high value on the vote and support of the congregation for certain decisions uniquely determining the future of the congregation. This commitment comes from what was done by the New Testament church itself.

Martin Bucer writes,

Since . . . people are weak and discipline and punishment are unpleasant, it is necessary that [pastors and elders] should as much as possible be trusted and respected by the believers among whom they are to serve the Lord.[7]

How true! Developing our congregation's trust will encourage their acceptance and growth through their elders' "discipline and punishment"— their correction, admonition, censure, and suspension from the fellowship around the Lord's Table. In the end, what do we desire more than the trust of the congregation for our discipline?

It is tempting for elders to forget they serve at the will of the people. This leads to elders becoming arrogant, lording their authority over the sheep they should love and care for tenderly.

This ought never to be.

It can happen for many reasons. We'll mention just a few to start readers down the path of avoiding this sin regardless of the way it might develop in their own congregations or their own hearts.

No Respect

Maybe the most typical pattern of high-handedness and lording authority over the sheep is the board of elders who have no respect for their moderator-pastor. This may have developed because the pastor is a jerk and they want him gone. It may have developed when a former pastor committed some serious sin that disqualified him from ministry, and after he left the elders came to wish they could hold all the authority and leadership themselves, not having to share it with some bum from the outside they don't know or trust. It may have developed because one of the elders is a wolf and views pastors as worthless human beings fit only to serve them as chaplains each Sunday and at important religious occasions such as baptisms, marriages, and deaths. Intimidated by the wolf, the other elders might fall in line behind him.

How does a board of elders despising their pastor cause them to be high-handed and to lord their authority over their congregation?

7. Bucer, 41.

There are many reasons, but certainly it makes sense that the sort of man who despises those above him will also despise those below him. We often caution young women that they should not consider a man for a husband who himself demonstrates no respect for or submission to authority. And oppositely, that if a man demonstrates respect and submission to authority, it's likely he'll not be a tyrant over her and their children.

Tragically, not a few congregations with Presbyterian polity have one elder who has climbed into the office, lords it over the pastor and congregation and his fellow elders, and has a tenacious grip on authority across the church. Often this man is known (or thought) to have a lot of money, so the church fears that removing him from office will leave the church high and dry without his financial support. The natural man thinks it is better to have a bad elder than to lose such an important source of income. Who can afford *that*?

Through the years, both of us have regularly experienced this situation in our congregations. One of us has experienced it twice, and in both cases it turned out the rich man actually gave very little.

It's painful to learn how much easier it is to allow a man to become an elder than to remove him. Congregations and pastors should select elders very carefully, and a key part of that selection is requiring every man promoted to this office to be placed there by vote of the congregation.

What should be done when it's too late and the church is under the oppression of high-handed, lordly, and grasping elders?

This is a very difficult matter. Usually the best hope is for the pastor himself as moderator to exhort, admonish, correct, and rebuke the elder himself, but this can be difficult when that elder despises the pastoral office or the pastor himself and he's intimidated the other elders into silence. Sometimes a pastor from another church can help by coming in and meeting with the pastor and elders, but those elders would be unlikely to seek such assistance if they sense this pastor is being brought in to challenge or rebuke them.

The thing is, God's flock must have good, faithful, and humble shepherds if the sheep are to persevere to eternal life. So pray and do what is necessary to rid your flock of your resident wolf.

The "B" Word

If the sheep are to accept admonition and rebuke from us, they must sense our humility, and one way for us to cultivate humility in our work is to submit important matters other than church discipline to the congregation for their vote. There are many important decisions that may properly be placed before the congregation for their approval or disapproval of the session's recommendation. Take, for instance, the budget.

It is good practice for a session annually to develop and vote to recommend to the congregation a budget for the next fiscal year. In one of our churches, that budget is presented to the congregation for their vote. Before that vote, the budget is developed by a session-appointed budget committee composed of mostly men, but also several CPAs who happen to be women. The committee has two elders, one of whom the session appoints as chairman, as well as a couple pastors, the church treasurer, and a deacon or two. By the time the committee concludes its work and presents a budget to the elders, a lot of time and effort have been spent developing that budget, so the elders are understandably loath to make major changes. One thing is left, though, which the budget committee leaves to the elders for their own action: the pastors' salaries.

As head of staff, the senior pastor makes recommendations for each pastor's salary and leaves the meeting for the elders to discuss his suggestions and amend or adopt them. The elders typically amend some of the recommendations of the budget committee, then adopt the budget as a whole and distribute it to the congregation for review prior to the upcoming annual congregational budget meeting.

At this congregational meeting, the senior pastor presides as moderator and all parts of the budget unrelated to pastors' compensation are discussed, beginning with the chairman of the budget committee giving explanations and answering questions. When it comes time for consideration of the pastors' compensation, another elder takes over as moderator, and all pastors and their wives leave the meeting. Each pastor's—including the senior pastor's—compensation package is fully divulged in print and on the screen at the front of the church, name by name.

The congregation acts by vote on the pastors' salaries prior to calling them back into the meeting, at which time the senior pastor takes over as moderator and the congregation votes on the budget as a whole.

Why have we described this process in such detail?

Look it over and see how careful we are to build the congregation's trust in the use of the Lord's tithes and our offerings each year. Note the care the elders take to allow a full and free discussion of the pastors' compensation without the pressure of pastors and their wives being present. Note also that the pastors' compensation is open to view, including how much the senior pastor gets paid. There's a reason our congregational meetings aren't acrimonious. Yes, the Lord has been kind to this church, giving them a sweet congregational unity. Part of that sweet unity, though, is the fruit of a principle of openness and the seeking of the congregation's consent which has been carefully cultivated by the elders for twenty-five years now.

Other Ways to Build Trust

Copy this, and not just with finances. Look for opportunities to build the congregation's trust in their elders. Don't just tell them good news, but also the bad news. If an officer of the church has confessed the sin of having abused children thirty years ago, explain the situation to the congregation so they know why he has been removed from the eldership. If the elders and treasurer have made a mistake in their estimate of the cost of some capital improvement, tell the congregation. Admit you were wrong and ask for their understanding. Don't hide mistakes. Don't hide sins that are likely to become public anyhow. And don't hesitate to ask the congregation's forgiveness when appropriate.

Also, pay attention to how the senior pastor submits to the elders in his recommendations for changes to the terms of call for the other pastors. On every level, leadership should humbly submit to those they lead, and the pastor is to set the example, just as he ought. It does happen that elders do not accept a senior pastor's recommendations, and recently, one senior pastor wasn't pleased when he was informed. But after many years of pastoral ministry, it has become increasingly evident to both of us that much of the pastor's moral capital with his session comes from being told no by them, and by submitting to it graciously.

The same is true of the elders with the congregation. Submitting to the debate on the floor of the congregational meeting and doing so graciously is a significant way elders build the congregation's trust for them—including debate on matters much more important than the adoption of a budget or capital expenditures. This builds the congregation's trust in the elders' acts of discipline, and what is more important than the congregation trusting the elders when they say no to one of their members?

Again, the principle is building trust by taking important decisions to the congregation for their discussion, debate, and vote. Bylaws changes. Denominational affiliation. Election of officers. The call of a pastor. Changing the name of the church. Buying a new church building. Building an addition. Doctrinal statements on contemporary challenges, such as the Christian doctrine of sexuality, and who will and will not be able to be married by one of the church's pastors. These and more matters can be properly placed before the congregation by the session, listening to the wisdom of the assembly of believers.

Note the participation of the members of the Jerusalem church in their consideration of the appeal for advice and counsel from Antioch. First, we read that when the Apostle Paul and Barnabas "arrived at Jerusalem, they were received by the church and the apostles and the elders." Then the matter was deliberated over by the apostles and elders with "much debate." Sounds like a good elders meeting, doesn't it? In time, the apostles and elders came up with a recommendation, but note who approved the proposal: "Then it seemed good to the apostles and the elders, with the whole church."[8]

In our rebellious time, we must work hard to cultivate the trust of those we lead. High-handed leadership doesn't build trust. Respect the prayers, wisdom, and discernment of your congregation. Submit yourselves to them.

8. Acts 15:4, 7, 22.

But if you bite and devour one another, take care that you are not consumed by one another.

—*Galatians 5:15*

CHAPTER 6

Conflict

YOU MAY HAVE NOTICED IN THE PRECEDING
chapters how much of an elder's work presupposes conflict. Let's
talk a bit more about that.

Many of us think conflict does not belong in the Church of Jesus Christ.
Even worse, many of us think if there is conflict in a church, then the pastor
and elders have failed.

This is not biblical. It is true that we should work towards restoring and
maintaining peace within the church, but that peace must be the peace of
God, and conflict is often required to restore and maintain God's peace.
Look at the history of God's people. From Moses and the Prophets to the
Book of Acts and the Epistles, Scripture is one history of conflict. Conflict
is often the means God uses to reveal His truth to His people.

Conflict in Acts

Consider the Book of Acts. Chapter 5 tells us about a man and his wife
who pretended to give their fortune to the church while secretly keeping
some of it for themselves. The Apostle Peter confronted the man, then his

wife; their lies were exposed and their lives were forfeit, leaving the church in awe and fear of God.

Chapter 6 has a report about a conflict over food distribution in the church. Some suspected the Hebrew widows were not receiving their fair share. The apostles responded by instituting the office of deacon, thus resolving the conflict.

Chapter 11 records that, after preaching the Gospel to and baptizing the household of the Roman officer Cornelius, the Apostle Peter was confronted by the Jewish Christians in Jerusalem for dealing with Gentiles. Peter defended God's sovereignty, thus preparing the church for the coming mass evangelization and ingathering of the Gentiles to the household of faith.

In the previous chapter, we mentioned the conflict found in Acts 15 over whether or not Gentiles who believed in Jesus must be circumcised before they could be admitted to the church. The church of Antioch, where this debate first arose, sent a delegation to the church of Jerusalem. There, a council of apostles and elders hotly debated the issue. Eventually, the council issued a regulation freeing the Gentiles from the obligation to be circumcised and spelling out the requirements for them to join the church. The Jerusalem church instituted councils as a way of solving conflicts over doctrinal matters.

In his letter to the Galatians, the Apostle Paul recounts how he publicly confronted the Apostle Peter in Antioch when Peter had separated from the Gentile believers there.[1] This confrontation clarified the issue for both the Gentiles and the Jews there in that congregation.

Acts 15 tells us about a conflict between Barnabas and Paul, formerly close companions in the mission field, over their younger co-worker, John Mark. Here, the contention arises over the behavior of a man. It was not an issue of doctrine, as in the previous instances, and as a result, Paul and Barnabas separated. But later, we see Paul caring for Barnabas and his financial well-being.[2] In time, we find John Mark standing with Paul in his imprisonment in Rome, from where Paul commends Barnabas to the Colossian church.[3] Writing to his co-worker Timothy, Paul called John Mark "useful"

1. Galatians 2:11ff.
2. 1 Corinthians 9:6.
3. Colossians 4:10.

and asked Timothy to bring him along to himself.[4] Thus we learn that, in the Christian church, personal conflicts exist, and they can be overcome.

Finally, in Acts 21, we read how the apostles and Jerusalem elders carefully and wisely dealt with the conflict in the church caused by the news about Paul's mission among the Gentiles. The Apostle Paul submitted to their demands to make peace with his critics in the church, demonstrating his respect for the Jewish customs. This, then, became the cause of his journey to Rome, bringing the Gospel to what was then the capital of the world.

Conflict in the Epistles

Even a cursory reading of Paul's epistles indicates how constantly he was dealing with conflict in the young churches. There was every form of disorder and conflict in Corinth. There was the Galatians' desire to return to salvation by the works of the Law rather than salvation by faith in Jesus Christ alone. Paul called the Ephesians to live in unity and to mutually submit to proper authority.

What do you think? Did Paul one day sit down thinking, "Hey, I could write to my Ephesian friends. Unity and togetherness in submitting to authority would be cool subjects."

Certainly not! The Apostle Paul wrote because he had heard of dissension and rebellion in that church, and the same is true for the first letter of Peter and for Paul's letters to the churches in Philippi, Colossae, and Thessalonica. In 1 Thessalonians 5:12, he urges that church to "appreciate those who diligently labor among you, and have charge over you." Would he have written that without a concrete reason? He goes on, calling them to "live in peace with one another," and to "admonish the unruly"; then, later, to "keep away from every brother who leads an unruly life."[5] He must have known of strife and rebellion in the church there in Thessalonica.

Turning to the Apostle Paul's letters to Timothy and Titus, we find plenty of advice to these young men for how to deal with conflict and rebellion in the churches. To Titus, he writes that overseers should "be able both to exhort in sound doctrine and to refute those who contradict." He then explains why:

4. 2 Timothy 4:11.
5. 1 Thessalonians 5:13, 14; 2 Thessalonians 3:6.

For there are many rebellious men, empty talkers and deceivers, especially those of the circumcision, who must be silenced because they are upsetting whole families, teaching things they should not teach for the sake of sordid gain.[6]

This passage shows it is the job of elders to deal with such people.

Note that the Lord used all these situations to develop the theological foundations of His Church. We would be clueless how to deal with conflicts today if the apostles had been squeamish about dealing with them in their time.

In sum, don't be disheartened when conflict arises in your congregation. You stand in a long tradition. What matters is to address conflicts wisely so the church can grow in faith and unity.

Two Kinds of Conflict

This requires, first of all, that you realize there are good conflicts and bad conflicts. Bad conflicts are caused by pride, hardened hearts, disrespect, and foolish thinking. They are the result and the expression of what the Apostle Paul calls rebellious behavior. Bad conflicts must be addressed by church discipline, the aim of which is peace and reconciliation. Paul's own experience with Barnabas and John Mark illustrates that this is possible. (We will have more to say about church discipline in chapter 9.)

Good conflicts arise over issues of doctrine and church practice. Good conflicts provide opportunities for learning and spiritual growth. Elders can and should use them to the benefit of their churches. To paraphrase an old adage, "Never let a good conflict go to waste."[7]

The Presbyterian Church in America's Book of Church Order requires pastors and elders who are about to be ordained to first answer a number of questions. The PCA's 1973 version of these questions asked this: "Do you promise to be zealous and faithful in maintaining the truths of the

6. Titus 1:7, 9–11.
7. "Never let a good crisis go to waste." Commonly attributed to Churchill, although it is uncertain whether he ever said it.

Gospel and the purity and peace of the Church, whatever persecution or opposition may arise unto you on that account?"[8]

This question has been consistent across American Presbyterian books of church order since 1838. Purity is a matter of truth. The purity of the church is her faithfulness to the truth of the Bible. The peace spoken of here is neither the motionless silence of a cemetery nor the forced denial of any conflict. It is divine peace which testifies to itself through good and fruitful relations among the people in the church.

How do purity and peace relate to each other?

Bad Conflict

Bad conflict often comes with lies. Rebellious people spread lies about the elders and the pastors whose authority they wish to subvert and destroy. When it comes to bad conflicts, pastors and elders often have to reveal the truth about the rebels to the congregation as part of the process of church discipline. You cannot build peace in the church on lies. Jesus once told his disciples: "There is nothing covered up that will not be revealed, and hidden that will not be known."[9] Sooner or later, what has been covered up will become known to the church, and then the damage to the authority of the elders is greater than if they had told it early on. Doing so requires courage and faith.

Consider these words by Pastor John Bunyan:

> You must not only choose men of counsel; but if you would design the unity and peace of the churches, you must choose men of courage to govern them; for as there must be wisdom to bear with some, so there must be courage to correct others; as some must be instructed meekly, so others must be rebuked sharply, that they may be sound in the faith; there must be wisdom to rebuke some with long-suffering,

---

8. See Paragraph 5 of ch. 21, "The Ordination and Installation of Ministers," *The Historical Development of the Book of Church Order*, PCA Historical Center, accessed June 22, 2020, https://www.pcahistory.org/bco/fog/21/05.html. The PCA has since added the word "unity" to the historic words "purity and peace."

9. Luke 12:2.

and there must be courage to suppress and stop the mouths of others.
The apostle tells Titus of some "whose mouths must be stopped," or
else they would "subvert whole houses" (Titus 1:11). Where this courage
hath been wanting, not only whole houses, but whole churches have
been subverted. And Paul tells the Galatians, that when he saw some
endeavour to bring the churches into bondage, that he did not give
place to them, "no, not for an hour" (Galatians 2:5). If this course had
been taken by the rulers of churches, their peace had not been so often
invaded by unruly and vain talkers.[10]

There is no peace without truth.

Good Conflict

The relationship between truth and peace is different when it comes to
good conflicts. Good conflicts are a way to find out God's truth.

> "For My thoughts are not your thoughts,
> Nor are your ways My ways," declares the LORD.
> "For as the heavens are higher than the earth,
> So are My ways higher than your ways
> And My thoughts than your thoughts."[11]

Our human brain is too limited to understand the truth of the Word of
the Lord and what God does.

We can only grasp small kernels of His truth. Each of us typically grasps
a different kernel. This means that, together, we must struggle to perceive
as much of His truth as possible. We often go into a situation with a firm
perception of God's truth, only to find that others see it differently. Who
is right and who is wrong?

We have to enter into argument in order to find out. Each of us has to
explain what he perceives to be the truth. We compare our arguments, try
to put as many different aspects together to get a larger picture, sharpen
some arguments and reject others. Each of us brings his own history and

10. John Bunyan, "An Exhortation to Peace and Unity," *The Works of John Bunyan*, ed. George
Offor (Blackie and Son, 1859), 2:752.
    11. Isaiah 55:8–9.

practical experience into this process. What has worked elsewhere? What has hurt me in the past? Each of us brings his own convictions, which are sometimes very dear to us. Giving them up is hard, and so we fight for them.

Still, such fights can be fruitful as a way to come closer to God's truth together—if, that is, we engage in them with the humility that comes from knowing that our understanding is necessarily limited. As Proverbs 27:17 says, "Iron sharpens iron, so one man sharpens another." Sharpening iron requires strength. Sharpening one another is often painful. But if we do it humbly, the result will be good. Peace will result from it. We'll all come to a better understanding of the truth together, allowing each of us to give up old prejudices and convictions as we are unified in the truth we have attained.

This sounds sweet, but mind you, it requires courage. Elders are often reluctant to go into what they see will be a long argument. It's late in the evening, and who wants to keep going for another hour? The wisdom of the moderator is also particularly necessary. Pick your conflicts wisely. Don't struggle over every detail, or you might wear down the elders. But do not let opportunities for good conflicts pass by when you think that they can strengthen the quality of the congregation's purity and peace.

The Worst Thing Elders Can Do

Of course, good and bad conflicts are not always neatly separated. Sometimes, someone will raise an issue that seems doctrinal, but in the end turns out to be only personal. Dealing with such cases requires even greater wisdom.

Keep in mind, though, that the worst thing elders can do is neglect an issue of doctrinal truth in order to avoid a conflict with an individual or group in the church. As John Calvin warns us in his commentary on Acts 15:2,

> "Peace" is certainly a pleasing word; but cursed is the peace that is obtained at so great a cost that there is lost to us the doctrine of Christ, by which alone we grow together into a godly and holy unity.[12]

12. Calvin, *The Acts of the Apostles 14–28*, trans. John W. Fraser, vol. 7 of *Calvin's Commentaries*, ed. Torrance and Torrance (Eerdmans, 1966), 27.

A little leaven leavens the whole lump of dough.

—Galatians 5:9

CHAPTER 7

Guarding the Flock

WE TURN NEXT TO THE ELDER'S RESPONSIBIL-
ity to protect the flock. As a whole.

In our individualistic age, it must be emphasized that this duty comes before the elder's duty to protect individual sheep.

The flock is more important.

More important? How can we say this? Don't individual sheep matter? Isn't the elder to follow our Lord in going out from the flock to find that one lost sheep? Haven't we said the real test of a man's love is not what he tells you about his love for humanity, but what he does to serve individuals?

Yes and yes, but even the protection of individual sheep first requires the protection of the flock.

It's simple. A shepherd cannot go out from the flock unless the flock is in good condition and well-protected. Furthermore, the flock must always have the elders' first attention and most rigorous defense, because the flock—the Church—is the Bride of Christ, and therefore His name and honor are at stake when the flock is in bad shape.

A Long Tradition

In this connection, note that, from the early Reformers on, the honor of Christ is preeminent in the explanations of the necessity of church discipline given by our fathers in the faith. Take, for instance, this list of the "ends" (purposes) of discipline given by John Calvin:

> In [church discipline], the church has three ends in view. The first is that they who lead a filthy and infamous life may not be called Christians, to the dishonor of God. . . . For since the church itself is the body of Christ, it cannot be corrupted by such foul and decaying members without some disgrace falling upon its Head. . . .
>
> The second purpose is that the good be not corrupted by the constant company of the wicked, as commonly happens. . . . The apostle noted this tendency when he bade the Corinthians expel the incestuous man from their company. "A little leaven," he says, "ferments the whole lump" (1 Corinthians 5:6). . . .
>
> The third purpose is that those overcome by shame for their baseness begin to repent. They who under gentler treatment would have become more stubborn so profit by the chastisement of their own evil as to be awakened when they feel the rod. The apostle means this when he speaks as follows: "If anyone does not obey our teaching, note that man; and do not mingle with him, that he may be ashamed" (2 Thessalonians 3:14).[1]

Both Presbyterian and Baptist Puritans made these same points. For instance, here is seventeenth-century London Baptist pastor Benjamin Keach:

> Because [a person's] Sin is open and scandalous, he ought to be cast out to vindicate the Honour of Christ and the Church, as part of his just Punishment . . . as well as to bring the Person to thorow Repentance.[2]

---

1. *Institutes* 4.12.5.
2. *The Glory of a True Church, and Its Discipline Display'd* (1697), Early English Books Online Text Creation Partnership, accessed March 8, 2019, https://quod.lib.umich.edu/e/eebo/A47522.0001.001?rgn=main;view=fulltext.

Read other historical Protestant summaries of the nature and purpose of church discipline and it will always be stated clearly that the highest purpose of discipline is not the restoration of the individual sinner but the protection of the flock—and this both to vindicate the honor of Christ and to keep contagion out of the whole. Thus this from the Westminster Confession of Faith:

> Church censures are necessary, for the reclaiming and gaining of offending brethren, for deterring of others from the like offenses, for purging out of that leaven which might infect the whole lump, for vindicating the honor of Christ . . .[3]

Here, the order is inverted: from the lesser to the greater, from the individual to the congregation.

Similarly, back in 1774 here in North America, a Baptist book on church order is concluded with this list of the purposes of church discipline:

> 1. The glory of God . . . is the ultimate end of it; for as his name is dishonoured by the evil practices or principles of church-members, so this is the most open and most effectual way of removing that dishonour that is brought upon it . . . — 2. Another end is to purge the church, and preserve it from infection; a little leaven leavens the whole lump, and therefore the old leaven must be purged out . . . — 4. . . . for the saving of the souls of men; . . . who are hereby brought to shame and repentance for their sins . . .

Again, first and foremost among the elders' concerns must be the well-being of the flock as a whole—their entire congregation.

Here is a story from the records of one of our churches. A few years after it had been founded, the elders reprimanded a man who was one of the founders of the church. The reason was that he had been repeatedly observed walking home while singing drinking songs loudly in the streets. Quite obviously, he had been drinking too much. The people in

---

3. Westminster Confession of Faith, 30.3, accessed June 22, 2020, http://clearnotesongbook .com/confessions/westminster-confession-faith-1646.

the neighborhood knew him, and they knew he was among the founders of that church. Naturally, they made jokes about the church—what kind of church had founding members who were commonly seen drunk?

The elders warned this man. Then, after a couple of warnings had failed to bring him to repentance, he was expelled from the church. The records give the official reason for the elders' action: "Because such behavior publicly violates the honor of the Lord Jesus Christ!" (More of this story at a later point.)

Let's break down the threats against the flock as a whole. First, we'll look at threats from inside the church that cause the name of our Lord Jesus to be blasphemed by pagans.

Public Scandal

Here's another example from our pastoral work through the years.

I was a new pastor in the mainline denomination, the Presbyterian Church (USA). I had been at my first church a couple years when I got a phone call from one of our elders. She (yes, we had women elders then) was hesitant. I could tell the call pained her greatly. A good woman who loved Jesus much, she said she was sorry to tell me that our church had become the subject of conversations in the bars downtown. People were laughing at the church for nominating a certain woman as elder. They thought it was hilarious because this woman wasn't married to the man she was living with.

I knew this middle-aged mother well. I knew she lived with the father of her children, and that they ran a farm together. I knew their relatives, but being a newcomer to the community, I didn't know she and her man weren't married.

Shocked, I thanked the elder and said we should set up a meeting to talk to this woman. We met with her and told her about the bars downtown laughing at Christ's Church. I asked whether it was true that she wasn't married to her man.

She admitted they weren't married. Many years earlier they had divorced, but then quickly got back together. But they had never remarried.

Gently explaining the scandal, I asked her if she thought it would be right for a woman to be elected an elder if she was living with a man without benefit of marriage.

She said no. It would not be right. It would publicly dishonor the name of Jesus.

Our announcement of elder candidates preceded the election by quite some time, so several weeks passed during which I had occasion to go out and visit the mother of the man our elder candidate lived with. She also was a member of our parish. She and her husband shared a simple home out in the country, and this was my first visit. Our time was pleasant, and after a while I got up to leave.

As we were walking to the back door, the mother touched my arm and said, "By the way, that little thing about my son being married? You don't have to worry about it anymore."

A few days later, I told the woman who had warned me of the situation what the man's mother had said to me. I asked if she knew what had happened.

"Yes," she said, "they took a weekend and flew to Vegas and got married." That was that.

It's true one scandal was overcome while another went unaddressed. Specifically, this new elder who would exercise authority over the men of our congregation was a woman, and this is explicitly forbidden by God. We'll get to that prohibition elsewhere in the book, but for now let the point be made that the concern we expressed to this sister was the scandal it would cause for an elder of the church to be living in fornication.

If you had been sitting there with us, you would have heard us saying firmly that she would not be put forward as an elder candidate if she wasn't married. It would dishonor the name of our Lord Jesus Christ. The Bride of Christ needed to be protected from our deserved mocking by the heathen. The mockery could be cut off either by her standing down from nomination, in which case we could turn to the issue of correcting her as an individual (her husband wasn't a member). Or the mockery could be corrected by her getting married.

We made clear that she would not be voted on while living with a man she wasn't married to.

Now I realize this story is shocking. It's quite understandable that many readers can't quite get their heads around the condition of many small-town churches with all kinds of sins going on for generations left unaddressed by the pastor or elders. Taking up this call was a reform work I was committed to, and I'm pleased to report that, in time, the women of the parish stopped being willing to serve as elders—something they had been doing for decades. We all were blessed by many other wonderful works of the Holy Spirit there, and I still look back on that parish with gratitude to God that I was allowed to serve Him and His people there in that village.

The purpose of this story, though, is that the church as a whole must have our first attention.

The Honor of Christ

When Jesus cleansed the Temple, His primary concern wasn't the individual moneychangers and merchants who were stealing, but the honor of His Father, which was being trashed by these men. Thus, as He swung His whip and overturned the tables, this was His condemnation: "It is written, 'My house shall be called a house of prayer'; but you are making it a robbers' den."[4]

His concern was the honor of His Father's house.

Today, it is the honor of Jesus Christ which is at stake with the Church. This theme is constant across Scripture. Think of the hundreds of places where God's name and reputation are the basis for the prayers of the leaders of God's people. Following the idolatry and immorality of the sons of Israel around Aaron's golden calf, God told Moses He would wipe Israel out and make Moses the beginning of a new people of God.

But Moses responded by appealing to God to consider His own reputation:

> Now if You slay this people as one man, then the nations who have heard of Your fame will say, "Because the LORD could not bring this people into the land which He promised them by oath, therefore He slaughtered them in the wilderness."[5]

4. Matthew 21:13.
5. Numbers 14:15–16.

When it came to the welfare of the Old Testament church, God's name and honor were at stake. Moses argued this with God, and it caused God to relent. This theme of the reputation of God being bound up with His people is repeated throughout Scripture. In the Book of Acts, when the Church is persecuted, this is how God's people prayed: "Lord, take note of their threats, and grant that Your bond-servants may speak Your word with all confidence . . ."[6]

The unbelievers in our town were laughing at the Church of Jesus Christ because of the notorious sin in our congregation. It had to be dealt with firmly by silencing their mockery through cleansing our own conduct and morals.

The most famous example of this situation in Scripture is the incest in the church of Corinth dealt with by the Apostle Paul in his first letter to the Corinthians. Speaking of the terrible scandal of this sexual perversion existing in the midst of the Corinthians' smugness and pride, the Apostle Paul rebuked them by writing that this sin among them was "immorality of such a kind as does not exist even among the Gentiles."[7]

Never forget that the honor of Christ is at stake with the reputation of the church in front of the watching world.

Next, let's look at threats from inside the church that cause schism or division within the congregation itself.

Schism in the Church

The Apostle Paul is very concerned to exhort Titus to protect his congregation from schism:

> Reject a factious man after a first and second warning, knowing that such a man is perverted and is sinning, being self-condemned.[8]

"Factious man" here translates the Greek phrase *hairetikon anthrōpon*, and this is the single occurrence of any derivative from the Greek word *hairetikos* in the New Testament. We get our English words "heretic" and

---

6. Acts 4:29.
7. 1 Corinthians 5:1ff.
8. Titus 3:10–11.

"heresy" from this Greek word. Other versions of Scripture translate it "person who stirs up division," "divisive man," "sectarian," or "schismatic." Note the relatedness of the English words "schism" and "heresy." Both cause division in the church. Both destroy the church's unity, purity, and peace.

The Apostle Paul's intensity dealing with this threat to the Body of Christ is indicated by his use of numerical values. In schism, as in baseball, it's three strikes and you're out. Warn a divisive man only twice; then, if those two warnings are not sufficient to cause him to cease his attempts to divide the church, no more warnings—remove him from the church. Elders and pastors are to demonstrate zeal in protecting the flock from those who seek to divide it.

There was a man in one of our churches who belonged to the founding members. He was relatively rich and in an elevated position in his little town, and he devoted a lot of time and energy to this church. He had even passed his truck-driver test so he could haul around equipment for the church building (a remarkable thing for an academic). He had been an elder for many years and was still very influential among the members of the church. The sad thing was that he also had a very quarrelsome spirit. Whenever and wherever there was strife and dissension in the church or town, he was in the middle of it. Many had been hurt and disturbed by him, and many had turned their backs on the church because of him. But alas, because he was a founding member and because he had money, no elder and no pastor had ever dared to hold him accountable for the damage he had done.

When Jürgen finally did, immediately the man's ire turned against him. He began to slander the pastor, criticizing his preaching and his lack of proper style and experience. In a variety of ways, he obstructed the work of the church. He gathered a group of people around him and began to oppose the elders and the pastor at congregational meetings. Jürgen finally told him at a meeting with him and an elder that he would have to stop being divisive or leave the church.

A very ugly fight ensued, during which the man wrote letters to the members of the church falsely accusing the pastor of all sorts of things. Eventually, however, the man left, knowing that he would be formally expelled otherwise. The church regained its peace and unity and was able to begin enjoying a sweet fellowship.

But the story did not end there. Several months after he had left, the man was diagnosed with a fatal disease that caused him to pass away within a few weeks. Before he died, he called Jürgen and asked for a meeting. That meeting turned out to be most moving and sweet. Knowing his condition, the man asked for forgiveness and reconciliation so that he might die in peace. He petitioned that his wife be allowed to return to the church and have a spiritual home there. She came back as a faithful member.

Elders must confront divisive men and women in the church to preserve peace and to protect the sheep against destructive behavior. When they do not, they themselves become guilty of the damage the divisive person causes. In fact, had the elders and previous pastors confronted the man in time, he himself might have enjoyed a longer and happier life. Confronting schism is not only an act to protect the flock; it is also an act of care for the benefit of the divisive person.

Sweet Relief

There was a couple in one of our congregations who, for many years, had been plagued with sins and weaknesses that kept the pastors and elders busy. For years they received careful pastoral care from our church officers and their wives. Love covered a multitude of sins, and hard work was done coming alongside them in their lives and the lives of their children. Often this couple was at the center of conflicts of one sort or another, but things got worked out—until the next time.

Eventually, our officers and wives grew weary and even sometimes exasperated. It's hard to keep warning sheep for the same errors and sins without thinking about giving up on the warnings, but our leaders plugged on. For personal reasons, I had a soft spot in my heart for the father, and the other officers knew it.

But then it came to an end.

One day when I was out of town, I called one of our officers to ask how the session meeting had gone the previous night.

He answered that they had voted to file charges against the father of this family. Honestly, hearing of their action was a great relief. It was time to bring matters to a head, and we all knew it.

What had caused the session to proceed to formal discipline?

The family's weaknesses and sins had coalesced until, finally, they began fomenting schism through lying. Protests, complaints, and evasion had finally borne the fruit of them telling lies about another man in the church with the aim of that man and the session being at odds. They had long been schismatic and should have been disciplined years before. A good argument can be made that we had refused to obey the Apostle Paul's command of once, twice, and done. I certainly learned from all those years, and I don't think it's accidental that I now have an understanding of the Apostle Paul's numerical values concerning dealing with divisive men that I didn't have earlier in my ministry.

Yet the plain fact was that this was the first time this man's behavior had been so very clear and so easily documented.

So we proceeded to hold a trial with witnesses called to testify. Sadly, the man refused to obey the elders' summons to the trial. The trial was then held in his absence, but even at the conclusion of the trial, the man refused to come to hear his censure, and then to honor that censure. Instead, the man took his family out of the church and proceeded to do great harm to the church by lying about the elders and their discipline.

What's important, though, is that, with their departure, the church began to enjoy a very sweet peace within her fellowship. Because of this discipline of this divisive brother, the church began to enjoy the unity that Jesus asked of His Father in His great High Priestly Prayer:

> I am no longer in the world; and yet they themselves are in the world, and I come to You. Holy Father, keep them in Your name, the name which You have given Me, that they may be one even as We are.[9]

Now there's something noteworthy in this example. Removing this divisive man caused outsiders to speak evil of Christ's Church. When he left,

---

9. John 17:11.

this man slandered the church, and most of those who listened believed what they heard. In the previous example concerning the woman nominated to be an elder, it was people in the community speaking evil of us that we sought to avoid, whereas in this case it was our actions protecting the unity of the church that led to the church getting a bad name among outsiders. Should we have taken this likelihood into account and deferred their discipline indefinitely?

This is often the tack taken by sessions. It is often the case that our desire not to be spoken evil of by those we discipline causes us to avoid the hard work of church discipline.

But clearly, what the session did was right. Avoiding outsiders speaking evil of the Body of Christ should never lead the session to disobey this very specific command of God to remove the divisive man after two warnings. We must trust God with our reputation, or we'll never do what He commands, and thus we'll never have unity and peace in our fellowships. Just before His passion, Jesus prayed for the Church's unity. To Him it is precious. It's hard to overvalue church unity.

Doctrine Divides

We've looked at the elders' responsibility to remove notorious sin from inside the church that is causing outsiders to blaspheme the name of the Lord. We've looked at the elders' responsibility to remove divisive men from the church in order to protect or restore the church's unity.

We've had one example in which the divisiveness was caused by a lust for power and influence which, sadly, exists in many churches and often comes from people with money or with a significant role in the history of the local church. This sin is as old as the people of God. Witness the rebellion of Korah against Moses,[10] as well as the many other instances of murmuring against him. Murmuring is a particularly vicious form of divisiveness, because it is difficult to keep track of and find the individuals behind it. Elders need to watch for that.

In the immediately preceding example, this divisiveness was a matter

10. See Numbers 16.

of lies told by one brother against another. But there's another category of divisiveness that is not a matter of behavior, but doctrine, and this needs our attention also.

Much of the content of the Epistles is the apostles' work to restore the Church's unity by opposing and removing doctrinal threats.

The first thing to keep in mind about doctrinal threats is that they are usually subtle. Being insidious, they are much harder to deal with than a woman living with a man she's not married to or a man lying about another man in the congregation. It's for this reason that the Epistles weave exposures of the schismatics' motives and character in among exposures of their denials of God's truth.

Now hold steady because this one might hurt. As an elder, never defend God's truth by studiously avoiding thinking or speaking about the character of the man attacking it. Doing so is a fool's errand. You will never be a good elder until you make your peace with appearing to the sheep as if you're being mean to those schismatics who are attacking God's truth. An elder cannot be squeamish about how he defends God and His Word, as well as Christ's precious Bride.

Our prime example could be our Lord Himself. Look at the chapters of the Gospels recording His attacks on the character of the church leaders scheming to murder Him. "Brood of vipers," "whitewashed tombs," "sons of hell;" stuff like that.[11]

Also consider how the Apostle Paul fights for the unity of the Church in his letter to the Galatians. One example will suffice. Speaking of the Judaizers in the Galatian church, he warns the Galatians, "They eagerly seek you, not commendably, but they wish to shut you out so that you will seek them."[12] In the midst of theological diagnosis and correction, the Epistles address and warn against the sinful character of the schismatics who are attacking God's truth.

Back in 1788, two geographical centers of American Presbyterianism, the Synods of Philadelphia and New York, composed and adopted as the introduction to their Form of Government what are still known and used today in American Presbyterianism—the Preliminary Principles. The fourth of

11. See for example, Matthew 23:33, 37, 15.
12. Galatians 4:17.

these principles has never left my mind since I first read it almost forty years ago:

> That truth is in order to goodness; and the great touchstone of truth, its tendency to promote holiness; according to our Saviour's rule, "by their fruits ye shall know them:" And that no opinion can be either more pernicious or absurd, than that which brings truth and falsehood upon a level, and represents it as of no consequence what a man's opinions are. On the contrary, they are persuaded, that there is an inseparable connection between faith and practice, truth and duty. Otherwise, it would be of no consequence either to discover truth, or to embrace it.[13]

Back in 1979, I had the privilege of working for a year as a pastoral intern at First Presbyterian Church in Boulder, Colorado. A number of things said by the senior pastor that year stuck in my mind, and as I write, I recall his statement during a pastoral staff meeting one week: "Every church has one or two men who are frustrated pastors, and they will cause a lot of problems."

By "frustrated pastors," he meant men who thought they should be pastors, but weren't. The wisdom of this warning has been evident to me throughout the years and I bring it up here because many of the doctrinal errors promoted by schismatics are bound to the desire of the heterodox and heretical to seek disciples who will follow them, turning away from their own elders and pastors. This is common in churches today. The schismatic wants men to follow him, and he teaches falsely in order to lead the sheep away from their fold and its shepherds.

You may not wish to think about this, since it's so very personal. After all, this man is trying to displace you and your fellow elders and pastor in the affection and loyalty of the sheep. You will have mixed motives as you deal with him, and even if you don't, others will accuse you of it. But, dear brothers, you must deal with it. If the Apostle Paul dealt forthrightly with it, and regularly, why should you refuse to? Yes, it's awkward, but is your congregation's unity worth protecting, or not? If you don't protect

---

13. Preliminary Principles, *Historic Documents in American Presbyterian History*, PCA Historical Center, accessed June 22, 2020, https://www.pcahistory.org/documents/principles.html.

God's flock, who will? Sure, your motives will be as misunderstood as the Apostle Paul's were, but silence isn't golden when you're the shepherd and wolves are snarling.

Of course you should suspect your own motives. Of course it could be you, your session, and your pastor who are wrong, and your critic who is defending the unity of the church and her orthodoxy. If so, humble yourself and repent.

On the other hand, if, to the best of your knowledge and study, it's the critic who is deviating from truth and working to build a schismatic base of followers with his teaching, you best get to work—and right away. Time's a-wastin'.

Finding the Right Balance

Finally, we must talk about wolves attacking the church from the outside. Every church lives in the tension between being open to outsiders who wish to come in and being closed in order to protect the flock. Some churches build high fences around themselves to ensure that no bad influences can enter and disturb their peace and purity. Others pull down the walls to assure that nothing hinders seekers from coming and finding Christ. The desire to protect the church is as good and valid as the desire to invite unbelievers and to grow the church. Wise elders find a balance between the two.

People who come in from the outside are likely to create some stir, especially if they come in large numbers. Most of the time, there is no bad intention involved on their part. They simply do not know the culture of the particular church, and they may not know much about the Christian faith or life as a Christian. They simply behave as they always do, and the problem may be that this behavior is very different from the culture of your church.

Think about smoking and drinking at church events, dress that might seem improper to the people who have belonged to the church for a while, or being overly jocular. Naturally, you do not want to correct such outsiders harshly, because they might turn away and not come back. But you also do not want to make those who have been in the church for a while feel uncomfortable—sometimes even perceiving themselves as being treated with a lack of respect.

Jürgen remembers how he first came to Indiana as an assistant professor at the local university. Being from Germany, he knew nothing about American manners, much less about how to behave in a conservative, Midwestern church. Fortunately, that church had wise elders and loving people. They welcomed him and his wife and, after a while, asked them to clean the bathrooms for the church.

Just fancy a German professor cleaning the toilets! The fact is, to this day, they are both thankful for this. It was the simplest possible job in the church they could get, one that required no cultural sophistication at all. And yet, it was a way of giving Jürgen and his wife a chance to contribute to the life of the church and be part of it, and it gave the church opportunities to thank them. The point is, give those who come from the outside little tasks so you can thank them, but do not give them a role in the worship team, the music team, or other works that require greater visibility and responsibility. Not before you have gotten to know them.

Another experience Jürgen had is more recent. When the huge wave of refugees came to Germany in 2015, the church where he was pastor suddenly filled with large numbers of Africans and Asians. Lovely people, but people with lots of needs, lots of questions, and no idea how to behave in church.

Initially, the older members were all excited about the newcomers. After a while, though, the murmuring began: "We don't count in this church anymore. They do what they want and we have to tolerate it all!" Three different cultures in a room are sure to create trouble. Things improved quickly by creating lots of opportunities to sit and talk and listen. The best reaction to murmuring against newcomers is not to chase them away, but to address and explain cultural differences and make it very clear that cultural differences are not the same as believing in a different God. Today, this church is an amazing community of very different people living together in unity and fellowship.

Some people, however, come into a church to cause trouble. There are notorious church-hoppers who come in, try to turn around the life and culture of the church as they like, and demand that everybody follow them.

Elders must stop such people. If they do not submit themselves to the church, they must be told to stay away.

Some people come into the church with an agenda of undermining its teaching and faithfulness to the Word of the Lord. Elders must oppose such people from the beginning. Once again, that may be difficult. Is that lady in the pink dresses that has come for a number of weeks a repentant trans-sexual, or is she looking for trouble? It takes prayer and careful observation to find out. But it is the elders' responsibility to make a proper judgment.

It is our good work to put ourselves on the line in protecting the Church's purity and peace.

Obey your leaders and submit to them, for they keep watch over your souls as those who will give an account. Let them do this with joy and not with grief, for this would be unprofitable for you.

—Hebrews 13:17

CHAPTER 8

Guarding the Sheep

NOW WE TURN TO THE ELDER'S DUTY TO CARE for the sheep. This duty differs from the elder's duty to guard the flock, because here he turns his attention from the group to the individual. It is the calling of the elder to watch over each family and individual—not just the flock as a whole. He is to give personal attention to households, whether blood-related or not, as well as those living alone.

Although the protection of the entire flock comes first in the elder's priorities, elders should not allow concern for the congregation to be their excuse for neglecting the hard work of knowing and caring for individual sheep.

It is a common sin in session meetings for elders to tell fellow elders of their great concern for "the church" while demonstrating little concern and no love for any individual sheep. But this is impossible. Love for mankind never rises above the love for individual men. Each of us, then, should test our concern for the Body of Christ by examining our concern for individuals within the Body.

If, during a session meeting, an elder argues strenuously for something

107

he claims is wanted by "the people in the church," but his fellow elders have long observed this elder's lack of hospitality or intimacy with families and individuals of the congregation, it's likely he's using his expression of concern for "the church" as a cover for his own personal desires—or perhaps the desires of his wife.

Don't allow stingy and selfish elders to use concern for "the people" as an excuse for pursuing his own agenda by controlling expenditures or other decisions. No one should be allowed to posture himself as the advocate for people he won't name because he doesn't know. Doing so undermines healthy discussion in the session, and it's the moderator's job to keep discussions and debate honest and healthy.

Again, men who claim love for humanity often demonstrate no concrete love for individuals. Concerning the elders of Christ's Church, we can't be firm enough about this. Once we have this category of hypocrisy in our minds, we'll begin to recognize it in ourselves and others.

Faithful in a Little Thing

Love is proven by its individuality and practicality. Concern and leadership are demonstrated in the small thing. As our Lord said, "He who is faithful in a very little thing is faithful also in much; and he who is unrighteous in a very little thing is unrighteous also in much."[1]

We see this principle in the listing of qualifications for the office of elder. Scripture commands that elders be men who have demonstrated their ability to manage their own household well. Why?

Because "if a man does not know how to manage his own household, how will he take care of the church of God?"[2]

Our Lord was so tender in His actions toward individuals. Think of His care for the Samaritan woman at the well. Think of His never-ending work healing individuals. Think of His tears for dead Lazarus and his mourning sisters. Think of His description of His own priorities concerning the sheep:

What man among you, if he has a hundred sheep and has lost one of

1. Luke 16:10.
2. 1 Timothy 3:5.

them, does not leave the ninety-nine in the open pasture and go after the one which is lost until he finds it? When he has found it, he lays it on his shoulders, rejoicing. And when he comes home, he calls together his friends and his neighbors, saying to them, "Rejoice with me, for I have found my sheep which was lost!"[3]

Think of Jesus' sensitivity to the hunger pangs of the souls who had gathered to listen to His teaching. He forbade His disciples to send them off to the village to fend for themselves.[4] Think of His rebuke of the disciples when they tried to get blind Bartimaeus to stop crying out for Jesus.[5]

When the disciples tried to shoo the children off, how did Jesus respond?

"Let the children alone, and do not hinder them from coming to Me; for the kingdom of heaven belongs to such as these." After laying His hands on them, He departed from there.[6]

"After laying His hands on them." Oh my! What father's heart is not warmed?

Mothers remember it was prophesied of our Lord:

Like a shepherd He will tend His flock,
In His arm He will gather the lambs
And carry them in His bosom;
He will gently lead the nursing ewes.[7]

Jesus never stopped loving and caring for individuals. Even when they turned away from Him, He loved them still.

For some elders, our desire to shepherd from a distance (shepherding the flock as a whole and not bothering with individuals) is driven by our fear of rejection. If you are a pastor or elder, examine yourself and see if you are

3. Luke 15:4–6.
4. Matthew 14:15–21.
5. Mark 10:46–52.
6. Matthew 19:13–15.
7. Isaiah 40:11.

willing to suffer the rejection of your sheep. How often is your avoidance of knowing your sheep simply your self-defense mechanism against all your fears? Maybe they'll reject your love? Maybe they'll think your questions impertinent? Maybe they want to be one in a herd rather than one in a flock? Maybe they'll mistake your intentions and think you're a busybody; or worse, a self-righteous moralist? Maybe they think you shouldn't be an elder? Maybe they voted against you?

Sure, the best way to avoid rejection is to avoid the sheep.

Jesus was despised, but this did not keep Him from loving individuals. He suffered their opposition and rejection constantly. This had been prophesied beforehand:

> He was despised and forsaken of men,
> A man of sorrows and acquainted with grief;
> And like one from whom men hide their face
> He was despised, and we did not esteem Him.[8]

The story immediately following Jesus' blessing of the children is the account of the rich young ruler. Knowing all things, Jesus was aware of the impending rejection of His pastoral counsel, yet something motivated Him to close with the man and speak tenderly to him about his soul:

> Looking at him, Jesus felt a love for him and said to him, "One thing you lack: go and sell all you possess and give to the poor, and you will have treasure in heaven; and come, follow Me." But at these words he was saddened, and he went away grieving, for he was one who owned much property.[9]

Loving Rebellious Sheep

At this point in our lives, both of your writers have been blessed by God with congregations whose members love and listen to their shepherds. The work of the elders of our two congregations is often joyful.

8. Isaiah 53:3.
9. Mark 10:21–22.

What would we counsel those whose sheep have no respect for elders, and thus refuse to heed their counsel and authority? Those who take elders for granted? Those who actually despise their elders?

Live by faith. We must buck up and do our work, looking to God for our reward. Both of us have had sheep who have despised and slandered us, both privately and publicly. But this is nothing new among pastors and elders. Consider the case of Charles Simeon.

Appointed by his father's friend, Bishop Ely, to the pulpit of Holy Trinity in Cambridge at the tender age of twenty-three, Simeon was despised by his congregation. Simeon had never served as a rector's assistant (curate), so when Bishop Ely placed him as the rector of Holy Trinity, Simeon jumped past all the curates in line before him. This included the Reverend John Hammond, the much-loved assistant to Simeon's predecessor whom the parishioners at Holy Trinity had petitioned Bishop Ely to appoint.

While the congregation had to submit to the bishop in his appointment of Simeon as their rector, they themselves had the right to hire a lecturer for the church, chosen and paid by subscription of the congregation's members. Promptly, then, Holy Trinity's parishioners appointed their former curate, John Hammond, to the lectureship, promising him double Simeon's annual salary. The lecturer held the right to officiate and preach a worship service each Lord's Day afternoon, so Simeon lived with Hammond conducting a competing worship service for the next five years.

But it wasn't just that his congregation preferred and attended another preacher each Sunday. On Sunday, November 10, 1782, the day after his appointment as rector, Simeon preached for the first time in Holy Trinity Church.

The churchwardens and . . . Church Council were infuriated. Their first reaction was to encourage all the regular pew-holders to fix locks on their pews so that, while staying away from the services themselves in protest, no one else could be admitted to their empty seats, thus leaving the preacher with a sea of vacant places before him. So those who did in fact wish to attend . . . had either to stand in the aisles or sit on benches in obscure corners of the church. When Simeon had further seats provided at his own expense, the irate and frustrated wardens showed their total lack of Christian grace by throwing them out into the churchyard.[10]

Several petitions for Simeon's removal were signed by ninety or more of his parishioners. Beyond Lord's Day worship, Simeon's challenges continued into his pastoral care:

> Unable to visit his parishioners in their own houses because they were so embittered against him, Simeon invited the faithful few to meet him for prayer and Bible study in a private room in the parish on a week-night evening. This room soon grew too small . . .[11]

What do we have to complain about? Pastors and elders have always suffered headbutts from the rams of their flocks. Our Master warned anyone who would follow Him that he would have to deny himself and take up his cross.

What we really must keep our thoughts centered on is not the opposition we suffer. Instead, let us ask ourselves what our Master will say to us when the time comes to give an account of our protection of His sheep.

Think of what Jeremiah suffered. Think of Jesus. Think of the Apostle Paul. Think of the obloquy and hatred that attended the ministries of men such as Charles Simeon, Jonathan Edwards, Charles Spurgeon, and Martyn Lloyd-Jones. Let the love of Christ dwelling in you cover over the disrespect and repudiation of your office, and get busy.

Love your sheep—the teachable, but particularly the unteachable. Love your sheep, both the submissive and rebellious. Love your sheep and do your work well, always by faith.

Let's turn to specifics. What are some areas where your sheep need your help and protection?

---

10. Hugh Evan Hopkins, *Charles Simeon of Cambridge* (Eerdmans, 1977), 38.
11. Ibid., 47.

Protecting the Sheep's Body

One area sheep need protection is their physical bodies. Few things are more spiritually destructive to our sheep than the sexual abuse and sin their bodies suffer at the hands of others. The Corinthian elders needed the Apostle Paul's help in this area, and any elder half-awake today knows our sheep need similar warnings, discipline, and protection.

Open Your Eyes

Despite being inundated by accounts of physical and sexual abuse committed by those in positions of authority, it's criminal how little discussion is paid this horror during our training and work as elders. Looking at specifics in our care for individual sheep, we start here.

As an elder, it is your duty to keep watch over your sheep, discovering and eradicating threats and crimes of abuse against their bodies.

But you ask, "How am I to know?"

Dear brother, it is your job to know. If I've learned one thing in our pastors' and elders' work with the abused and their oppressors, it is that the main problem the church and her officers face in guarding their sheep in this regard is not the hiddenness of these sins. Rather, the problem is our personal resistance to seeing what we see, and then to stepping in to break the jaw of the oppressor, snatching the sheep from him.[12]

At this point I can hear many protests. I've heard all the excuses before and have no patience for those who use them to justify themselves. Sorry for the strong words, but I'm no internet blabbermouth who hates authority and men. For thirty-five years I've served in the trenches getting dirty alongside fellow pastors and elders as we discover, expose, and bring to healing and justice those suffering from, as well as those perpetrating, physical abuse, sexual or otherwise. We also have much experience helping other churches' pastors and elders do the same within their congregations.

So I speak as a veteran, and the elders and other pastors of our congregation can as well. All of us will testify that the problem in the Church today concerning the epidemic of physical and sexual abuse we are suffering shame

---

12. See Job 29:17.

for in the eyes of the world is not that we didn't know of the sin. The truth is, we didn't want to know and avoided it.

No one's so blind as the man who doesn't want to see.

You may say it's not your job to search out the abuse in your congregation. But who is in a better position than you?—with the inestimably valuable help of your wife, of course.

Yes, your wife should be a godly extension of your pastoral care, gathering knowledge concerning the dangers threatening, and crimes tormenting, your sheep. If not, why isn't she?

Sure, there are things in your work she shouldn't know, just as there are things in her work you shouldn't know. But in the work of eldership (just as in the work of the pastorate), God made the two of you one. By God's design the man and his wife are a team, and what they are able to do together is much greater than what they could ever accomplish alone. This not simply because of the encouragement your wife gives you, but also because of the knowledge and advice she, as a woman, will bring to your work.

Men and women are different, you know. We know different things through our different ways of knowing. If it wasn't just Aquila, but also Priscilla who had knowledge to give as a help to Apollos,[13] how much more do our wives have knowledge we need in order to care for our sheep conscientiously and wisely?

Elders and their wives must be intimate with their sheep. Elders and their wives must know their sheep. The sheep must know their elders and their wives. They should feel safe standing next to their elders, being fed and protected by them. The godly wife strengthens her husband in his shepherding work. Too many elders have a wife whose zeal for her husband's care for the household ends with herself and her children, never extending to the well-being of the household of faith which is the Church of the Living God:[14]

> God has created the woman to be a help to the man and that they might
> live godly lives together. Therefore, when marriage has been entered

13. See Acts 18:24–26.
14. 1 Timothy 3:15.

on and continued in the Lord, the wife does not separate her husband from the Lord. And when the wife is also zealous for the kingdom of God, her husband will please her more not by neglecting the work of God, but by carrying it out faithfully and well.[15]

What a blessing it is when the godly husband and his wife together join in the work of the Lord, using their time, children, money, home, and talents to teach, strengthen, protect, and heal the sheep of God. What a tragedy when the men and women, boys and girls, of our churches feel safer with their physician or Christian counselor than with their elders and their wives. Pastors and elders should not pawn off on professionals the discovery of and protection of their sheep from abuse they are suffering in their own homes and families.

Fellow elder, God has called you and set you apart through the laying on of hands and prayer to the work of shepherding His flock. Like any good shepherd of sheep, it is your responsibility to keep your eyes open and watchful for threats to the souls and bodies of your sheep. And you may not neglect their bodies under the guise of zeal for their souls. God has made us body and soul, one man, and it is impossible to care for the soul without caring for the body.

This is what we see our Good Shepherd doing in His time here ministering on earth. When John the Baptist sent His disciples to Jesus to ask if He was truly the Messiah, Jesus responded,

Go and report to John what you have seen and heard: the blind receive sight, the lame walk, the lepers are cleansed, and the deaf hear, the dead are raised up, the poor have the gospel preached to them.[16]

The souls and bodies of our sheep are bound together inseparably, just as the Apostle James says:

If a brother or sister is without clothing and in need of daily food, and

15. Bucer, 48.
16. Luke 7:22.

one of you says to them, "Go in peace, be warmed and be filled," and yet
you do not give them what is necessary for their body, what use is that?[17]

Dear elder, we are our brothers' keepers, both soul and body. John Calvin's fellow reformer in Strasbourg, Pastor Martin Bucer, notes the connection between caring for the souls and bodies of God's sheep:

> Where the office of the care of souls is properly ordered and practised,
> we will not expect to see anything much lacking in this other ministry
> of care to the body.[18]

The particularities of the work of an elder are not science, but art, so
we don't want to weary you with endless instructions of what to do and
what not to do in this or that situation. Where there's a will, there's a way.

What to Look For

Now then, here are some thoughts about how to discover and respond to
the physical and sexual abuse of your sheep.

First, learn the signs of abuse and look for them within your flock.
You can't be equally responsible for every sheep of your congregation, but
some sheep you know better than others, and those sheep must receive
your careful attention.

For this reason our churches have put much emphasis on setting up
home fellowship groups.[19] They provide a wonderful opportunity to know
our sheep personally, both adults and children, and this is a great help in
our care for the sheep God has placed under us.

Regardless of how you order your congregation's life together, you need
to do so in a way that allows you to know your sheep. Here are some things
you want to look for:

17. James 2:15–16.
18. Bucer, 32.
19. Home fellowship groups at Trinity Reformed Church (where Tim serves) meet each Lord's
Day, most sharing a meal together. From the beginning over a decade ago, our participation rate has
been above ninety-five percent.

- Women who can't meet your eyes or the eyes of any man
- Wives whose faces are haggard and who rarely smile
- Children whose physical and emotional boundaries seem unhinged
- Children whose interaction with a parent or sibling seems flirtatious
- Children who engage in inappropriate or sexually precocious talk or play
- Fathers who joke or speak callously about their wife or children's bodies or sexuality
- Babies whose bottoms have bruises ▷ *As she works in the nursery, your wife is the one who could know this. When bruises are seen, it should not be assumed it's because of abuse. And yet, do the hard work and ask the questions.*
- Children who exhibit several obvious bruises ▷ *This may just be a rough-and-tumble kid, but then again, maybe the child's father or mother has a temper. Gently inquire. Probe. Sure, it's awkward, but what a small price to pay.*

In this critically important area of guarding your sheep against the abuse and incest at the center of the Corinthian church (for instance), our wives once again are such a help to our loving care as pastors and elders. They are the ones who will most naturally hear about, and see, such problems—for instance, as they obey Titus 2, teaching the younger women as God commands:

Older women . . . are to be reverent in their behavior, not malicious gossips nor enslaved to much wine, teaching what is good, so that they may encourage [teach] the young women to love their husbands, to love their children, to be sensible, pure, workers at home, kind, being subject to their own husbands, so that the word of God will not be dishonored.[20]

20. Titus 2:3–5.

As your wife teaches Sunday school, participates in the play group, and serves in the nursery, she has many opportunities to come to know the sheep and their lambs. She is your helpmate as you shepherd your sheep, so she should help you with the information you need to become a better shepherd of God's little ones.

You and your wife can also learn a lot through seemingly small things like discussions and prayer requests. Listen carefully to what might at first strike you as an insignificant comment. Don't miss the questions the sheep and lambs ask in Bible studies or other church gatherings.

Of course, we shouldn't run around on high alert looking under every nook and cranny for abuse, but you and your wife must know the warning signs, and when you see or hear them, take the necessary steps of loving care for others.

In Your Church—Really

Maybe you've been intimidated by this section and you're thinking to yourself, "We don't have any marriages or families like this in our church, so I don't need to worry about it."

Wrong.

Read your Bible. Read the session minutes of past centuries. Read the consistory records from Calvin's Geneva. Sins of abuse—both physical and sexual—are timeless and constant.

Read the specific reasons for which particular men and women were summoned to the weekly meetings Calvin and his fellow shepherds held each Thursday as they cared for their sheep in the churches of Geneva. Here are several from 1543:

Mathieu Canard because of murmuring.

. . .

Jehan L'Ostoz, weaver, why he left his wife in Lyon.

. . .

The wife of De Miribello because of murmuring at the sermons.

. . .

Claude, farm laborer, and Collete, his wife, . . . who beat each other.

. . .

Whether the children of De Pane have done with their mother what
the Council ordered last.

. . .

Angelline de Crouz, who does nothing but get angry at her daughter-
in-law and does nothing but insult her every day.

. . .

The son of Colleta Chabodaz, who is disobedient to his mother.

. . .

Mauris Savua, boatman, and his wife, who do not live together, and
she is said to fornicate and does not sleep with her husband. . . .

. . .

Marguerite, wife of a farm laborer who lives at Gruetz' house because of
her small child she left to die, which strangled itself in the cradle,
and she did not bother to go see it all day, and the neighbors
told her she should go to her child and she answered that it was
asleep, and it slept so much that she found it strangled.

. . .

Claude Moyron should be asked:
Whether he is married.
Whether he did not keep with his wife and his daughters a respect-
able girl who fornicated with him.
Whether he did not often beat his wife to effusion of blood because
she was sad.
Whether he did not threaten to beat his daughters if they said any-
thing about it. . . .[21]

Faithful elders have always guarded their sheep from abuse. Note particularly that these session records show men being disciplined as often as
women, and for the same things. Contrary to the feminists' slander, the
Reformers had no double standard for men and women five centuries ago.

The word "abuse" refers to actions and words that are sinful and enabled
by one's authority, so think of "abuse" as the "bad-use" of authority.

21. Selections from Robert Kingdon, Thomas Lambert, and Isabella Watt, eds., *Registers of the Consistory of Geneva in the Time of Calvin, Volume 1: 1542–1544*, trans. M. Wallace McDonald (Eerdmans,
2000), 424–432.

Now then, ask yourself: What word would properly be used to describe the shepherd of God's sheep and lambs who has reason to question the well-being of one of his flock, but turns away and forgets what he's just seen or heard?

Is this not the misuse of authority? The abuse, or bad-use, of authority?

Is it not abuse of authority when the elders or pastors refuse to use the authority God has delegated to them, but do nothing, acting as if they are ignorant of the suffering of their sheep? Is it not the very definition of a hireling or false shepherd that he acts as if he doesn't recognize the wolf and allows him free access to devour the sheep and lambs?

Remember that when Jesus described good and false shepherds, He didn't at that time speak of bad shepherds being dictators, or being egotistical men demanding their own way. What He warned against is shepherds who run away from the wolf,[22] and that's what we do when we refuse to watch out for, and fight against, the incest, molestation, and abuse in every last one of our congregations right now. You may not be able to find it, but don't be surprised or pull away from squeamishness when it finds you.

It's good that it finds you. After all, you're a shepherd. The sheep and lambs should come to you for protection. They should trust you to fight the wolf, just like Job:

> I broke the jaws of the wicked
> And snatched the prey from his teeth.[23]

After years working with the abused and helping to bring their abusers to justice, my wife and I put our own estimate of the people in the church who have been abused in the past, or are presently being abused, at somewhere around forty percent. Cut it in half if you like, but you're still looking at one in every five souls in your church having been raped, tormented, or attacked violently by an intimate enemy—often in their own home.

Do you want to answer to God for not watching and listening? For not defending your sheep?

Mothers sexually abuse their infants. Fathers physically and emotionally abuse their sons. Sisters sexually abuse their sisters and brothers. Priests

22. See John 10:12–13.
23. Job 29:17.

sexually abuse their parish's little boys. Pastors abuse the wives of the men of their congregations. Principals abuse the students of their classical Christian school. Choir directors force young men in their choirs to strip and submit to them beating their naked buttocks with an inch-and-a-half-thick wooden rod. And when these victims get the courage to ask their pastors and priests to help them escape their physical and sexual torture in their home, the pastor or priest responds by propositioning them sexually. Need I go on?

Do you really want this to happen on your watch? Do you love your tender and vulnerable sheep?

Protecting the Sheep's Soul

Here is Martin Bucer's summary of the work of pastors and elders:

> The five tasks of the care of souls [are] searching for and finding all the lost sheep, bringing back the strays, healing the injured, strengthening the ailing, and guarding the healthy ones and feeding them in the right way.[24]

We note the work is overwhelming in its scope and difficulty, but let us remember that we do not depend on ourselves. God has made us keepers of His sheep, and what God commands, He gives us the will, wisdom, and ability to obey.

We'll use Bucer's "five tasks" as an outline for what it means to protect the souls of our sheep.

1 *Seeking and Finding Lost Sheep*

Arriving at my previous church, I learned the elders never reviewed their membership list. They were unaware of the people of their congregation as they came and went. No names of the missing brought up in session meetings, no subcommittee reviewing the church membership list for souls who were absent or even moved on to another city, no inquiries of those souls whether they had found a new church home, no discussion of children of the church who had stopped attending. No searching for lost sheep, at all.

24. Bucer, 212.

As you would expect, the membership roll just grew and grew, since there was no mechanism among the elders for addressing anyone's absence.

When we moved to town and I started preaching, I found out that one of the men who had been a great encouragement to my wife and me during our candidate visits had stopped coming. Asking around, I found that he and one of the leading ladies of the church had been at odds over the decoration of the church, and she'd won. So he stopped coming. But his name didn't come up in the session meetings and the elders seemed oblivious to his absence. Would they have taken his name off the membership list after a while without going to him to ask why he was absent?

No, the church secretary did that. She wouldn't visit or inquire of him, you understand, but simply remove his name from the membership list. Which is to say, whatever was done to keep the membership roll of that church current was done by the church secretary. Which is to say, whatever names were removed from the membership roll of that church were removed by the church secretary. Which is to say, whatever disciplinary action was carried out by that church was carried out by that church secretary because, as I learned, the highest and only action of discipline ever carried out by that church was the administrative purging of their membership roll. By the church secretary.

Now let me stop here and say that this secretary was not in the slightest controlling, and it would never have occurred to her that her removal of any name from the church's membership roll and mailing list had been her usurping the elders' authority. She was working as hard as she could, seeking only to be helpful in keeping this and that list up to date, and one of her lists happened to be the membership list. Pity her. She had no direction otherwise and wanted to be faithful in her work.

Sessions should regularly review their membership rolls, assigning an elder or pastor to go out and search for the lost, name by name. If they've left town, you can call or send them a letter or email (not a text) explaining you've missed seeing them and are wondering if things are well with them. If they're still in town, a few minutes of discussion in the session meeting can usually bear the fruit of an explanation of their absence. Maybe she started dating an unbeliever and stopped attending the college ministry? Maybe he had a fight with his wife and moved out? Maybe they feel the pastor is not sympathetic to parents who send their children to public schools, and they are shopping around for a congregation more sympathetic to public education? Maybe the father was arrested for child abuse and they're ashamed to show up for worship? Such discussion will often also lead to consideration of how best to approach them, and who should do it; usually an elder or pastor in the best position to appeal to that particular soul.

Go out and seek the lost. Set up mechanisms and administrative responsibilities and redundancy to those responsibilities so that you, as elders and pastors, cannot escape noticing who is missing, then going out to search for them. In our congregation, it is a key part of both our pastoral staff and session meetings to discuss people who are missing or in need, name by name. We expect our elders and pastors to notice each Lord's Day who is missing, and to know why. This is not our effort to enforce strict conformity. We do not get tied up in knots when a family or individual is missing for a week or two, but we do love our brothers and sisters in Christ, so we keep track of them, noting when they're missing, and wondering why.

Is this so hard? If a shepherd searches for his one lost sheep, should the shepherds of God's flock not do the same?

2 Bringing Back Strays

Our goal seeking the lost should be bringing them back to the safety of the sheepfold. To the church and her shepherds. How to bring them back?

First, humility. When we meet with the straying sheep, we should start by asking if we have offended him somehow and if there's something we can do to make things right. This is, of course, assuming there is not an obvious cause of his straying such as the rebuke of the elders for his abuse of his wife, his failure to hold down a job, or his use of pornography. In such cases, begin there. To start the meeting by inquiring whether you or someone else have offended him is to avoid the obvious, which is never good leadership. If there's an elephant in the room, don't act as if you don't see it.

Be a peacemaker as you work towards the return of the straying. Often the cause of sheep straying is a simple misunderstanding, or even intentionally hurtful behavior on the part of an officer or member of the congregation. If so, a simple apology from you or someone else, if it is sincere, will cause the sheep's return—and joyful reunion.

Other times, there is no such simple solution, and the work of restoration will be time-consuming and require great patience. He may not be able to see his own sin or bitterness causing his straying, so it is your privilege gently to lead him into greater self-knowledge and repentance.

Regardless of the cause, do the work, helping to motivate yourself by remembering our Savior's statement pulling back the curtains of Heaven:

> I tell you that in the same way, there will be more joy in heaven over one sinner who repents than over ninety-nine righteous persons who need no repentance.
>
> . . . In the same way, I tell you, there is joy in the presence of the angels of God over one sinner who repents."[25]

3 Healing the Injured   /   4 Strengthening the Ailing

If you haven't read Iain Murray's splendid biography of Pastor Martyn Lloyd-Jones,[26] you should. It's long, but don't let that put you off. Few books have so inspired us to faithfulness in ministry.

One remarkable thing about this brother many in the United Kingdom still refer to simply as "The Doctor" is how his former calling as a physician strengthened him in his pastoral work. Take, for instance, his counseling.

Each Lord's Day following worship, Lloyd-Jones would meet with inquirers seeking his counsel. Rarely would these souls spend more than a few minutes with him, and even more rarely would the inquirer be invited to sit down.

It was not that Lloyd-Jones was impatient or lacked proper people skills, but that he had been a doctor and learned the importance of diagnostic skills and directness in the work of healing. Which is to say, like any good physician, he got to the point, and that point was never him.

A confession. My wife has a recurring admonition by which she loves me: "It's not about you."

What I've begun to learn as the years have flown by is how often my

25. Luke 15:7, 10.

26. Iain Murray, *D. Martyn Lloyd-Jones*, vol. 1: *The First Forty Years 1899–1939* (Banner of Truth, 1982), vol. 2: *The Fight of Faith 1939–1981* (Banner of Truth, 1990).

pastoral care is as much or more about me as it is about the soul I'm caring for. I wish I could say I've learned this, past tense, but I remain very much in the learning process—as my dear Mary Lee will attest. One of the ways this shows up is my propensity to get depressed and assume I have failed someone who is angry with the elders, or with the church, or with their small group, or even with God. Maybe if I preached better sermons on this or that subject, or maybe if I had been more encouraging to them last Sunday at the picnic, or had paid more attention to their teenage son, or visited him in the hospital when he had a hernia operation; maybe if I had read the book he gave me or . . . You get the drift.

What a doctor knows when a patient shows up for his appointment is that it's not about him. It's about the patient. Dr. Lloyd-Jones didn't waste time with small talk or work to demonstrate his sensitivity to the lives of his sheep by engaging them in discussions about their hobby or job or what university their daughter was attending and how she was liking it. He got to the point, which was healing the injured and strengthening the ailing.

What is the injury or ailment? This is the question at hand, so all our energy should be focused on diagnosis followed by some prescription to remedy the matter. Good physicians are not embarrassed to have us remove our clothes. They don't avoid asking intimate questions. This should be the pastors' and elders' model for dealing with spiritual injuries and ailments. Prod and poke and ask and suggest and listen. Most of all, listen. Forget yourself.

This is the most important advice we can give on being helpful to the injured and sick.

Yes, good shepherds have sympathy and empathy for the injured and sick, but we should never allow that sympathy and empathy to overwhelm our diagnostic and therapeutic work. The point is not to convince the sick sheep that you really care about him and wish him well. The point is finding out what is harming him and how he can be healed.

Yes, sometimes you must deal with spiritual hypochondriacs. There are always plenty of people who merely want time with the pastor or an elder, and they will manufacture ailments to get your attention and pity. Don't let them. Not every sheep needs a shepherd's personal attention right when he demands it.

5 *Guarding and Feeding the Healthy*

We will simply say, as regards protecting healthy sheep, that what was outlined above concerning physical and sexual abuse applies here also. Good shepherds study the diseases and dangers of sheep and are able to anticipate those dangers, taking steps to turn the sheep away from them; or sometimes, when the danger is a hungry wolf, the good shepherd sets out to kill the wolf before he gets close to his prey. At risk are the sheep of our flocks, and we should protect them from men who are wolves by fighting for the removal of those wolves from our flock.

If the shepherd neglects his healthy sheep, they won't stay healthy very long. Give attention to healthy sheep. Don't allow sick sheep to absorb you in their maladies to the neglect of the rest of the flock who are humbly and quietly grazing nearby.

Then, finally, feeding the healthy ones in the right way.

We are to choose the feed we give our sheep, making our choices carefully in light of their preferences and needs. Here there is a matter of some sensitivity we need to address.

One of the more frequent points of conflict between elders and pastors is this matter of the proper feed mixture needed by the sheep. Everyone has his pet doctrine he thinks should be addressed regularly in the church's preaching and teaching. Or, if not a pet doctrine, a pet system of preaching or teaching. The doctrine could be the evils of abortion, the blessings of fruitfulness, the evils of public education, or the blessings of God's covenants across Scripture. The pet system of preaching could be expositional or redemptive-historical. It could be ending each sermon with a Gospel appeal.

Of course, all these things should come up in the normal work of preaching and teaching across any congregation, but Spurgeon once lamented pet themes and systems by exclaiming, "Strange that a harp of thousand strings, should play one tune so long."[27]

If the pastor neglects the law of God and repentance, preaching only

---

27. "On the Choice of a Text," *Lectures to My Students* (Zondervan, 1954), 95. Spurgeon here plays on a line from a hymn by Isaac Watts, which reads, "Strange, that a harp of thousand strings/Should keep in tune so long!" (Isaac Watts, "Let Others Boast How Strong They Be," hymn 19 in bk. 2, *The*

grace and faith, that pastor is not feeding his flock "in the right way." Don't abandon the sheep by avoiding the matter in your conversations with the pastor (who might be one of your closest friends). Talk to him about his avoidance of the more difficult parts of Scripture. Pastors need elders to help us be faithful. Many of us are fighting off our fears all the time, and no one should be surprised that fear often leads us to get the feed mixture of our flock wrong.

It's always easier, and leads to more positive conversations in the church doorway, if we couch everything we say in terms of grace. We pastors may defend the imbalance of our preaching and teaching by condemning the call to holiness as "piety" and the preaching and teaching of God's law and repentance as "moralism." Don't let us. Call us back to faithfulness. The health and well-being—which is to say, the perseverance—of the sheep depends upon it.

Just as common in churches, though, is the tension between an elder and the pastor over what that *elder* judges to be the feed mixture needed by the flock. Be careful. This is where we need to return to the matter we addressed near the beginning of this book. Elders must respect their pastor, and it's the nature of the pastoral office that, in the final analysis, he is the one called and set apart by the Holy Spirit to carry the major responsibility of deciding the feed mixture. Scripture commands that he be honored "especially":

> The elders who rule well are to be considered worthy of double honor, especially those who work hard at preaching and teaching.[28]

A number of times I've had an elder or two come to me to critique my feed mixture for the flock. The one I remember best is an elder I loved very much who was so very helpful in so many ways, while being a terrible discouragement to me in my preaching. We met for lunch once a week for many years, and he invariably told me two things: first, that he'd never had

---

Psalms and Hymns of Isaac Watts, Christian Classics Ethereal Library, accessed July 2, 2020, https://ccel.org/ccel/watts/psalmshymns/psalmshymns.II.19.html)

28. 1 Timothy 5:17.

a pastor who loved his people as much as I loved ours; but then, second, without fail he'd go on to tell me that my preaching wasn't what the sheep (whom I loved so much) needed. Hundreds of times I listened as he said to me, "People's lives are hard. They just need to be encouraged."

Over and over and over for many years I listened as this dear and wise brother told me he had a better understanding than the pastor of the feed mixture the sheep needed.

It's a fine line between pushing your pastor to be faithful in difficult areas of preaching and teaching where he tends to pull back out of shyness or timidity and fear, and usurping his pastoral authority to set the feed mixture of the flock. Honestly, in the end, it's almost the center of all his responsibilities to know what feed mixture is best for his sheep, and to feed them that mixture. In fact, it's so central to his work that the session which concludes he's bad at it should ask him to move on or get a different day job.

If he's not able to feed the sheep "in the right way," what on earth is he able to do? Remember David's description of our Good Shepherd:

> The LORD is my shepherd; I shall not want.
> He maketh me to lie down in green pastures: he leadeth me
>   beside the still waters.
> He restoreth my soul: he leadeth me in the paths of righteousness
>   for his name's sake.[29]

The sheep cared for by the Good Shepherd Himself do not want, because He provides them green pastures and still waters, leading them in the paths of righteousness.

No, I do not deny that shepherds who are elders need to help shepherds who are pastors find and provide green grass and still waters, but be careful, because way too often elders telling the pastor what to, and what not to, preach and teach are, in fact, quenching the Holy Spirit. They are laying hands on God's anointed one, and not because he's wrong, but precisely because He fears God and loves the sheep and knows their perseverance in the faith depends upon his hard work to feed them what they need.

---

29. Psalm 23:1–3 (KJV).

To feed the sheep in the right way is to preach the full counsel of God. The Apostle Paul described his own feeding of the sheep this way:

> I did not shrink from declaring to you anything that was profitable, and teaching you publicly and from house to house, solemnly testifying to both Jews and Greeks of repentance toward God and faith in our Lord Jesus Christ. ... I testify to you this day that I am innocent of the blood of all men. For I did not shrink from declaring to you the whole purpose of God. Be on guard for yourselves and for all the flock, among which the Holy Spirit has made you overseers, to shepherd the church of God which He purchased with His own blood.[30]

Don't usurp your pastor's authority. Don't discourage him from being faithful. Help him.

---

30. Acts 20:20–21, 26–28.

All discipline for the moment seems not to be joyful, but sorrowful; yet to those who have been trained by it, afterwards it yields the peaceful fruit of righteousness.

—Hebrews 12:11

CHAPTER 9

Church Discipline

WE BEGIN THIS CHAPTER WITH A QUESTION:
Do you believe in church discipline?

The good reader naturally responds, "Of *course* I believe in church discipline!"

Well said, but maybe the question was answered too easily.

At this point the wiser among us might qualify his answer by inquiring, "What do you mean by 'church discipline'?"

Good question. This chapter on "church discipline" is not simply about formal disciplinary processes which have various formal outcomes up to and including excommunication. Church discipline is certainly those things, but an awful lot more of church discipline is of a less formal nature. We'll get back to the various forms of church discipline in a bit, but for now let's say we're only asking our leadoff question about formal process and the resultant admonitions, censures, and suspensions from the Lord's Table fellowship.

Willing to Work

Mary Lee and I were in Wisconsin being interviewed by the search committee of the two-church parish we hoped would issue our first call. This yoked parish had been sharing pastors for seventy years or so. One of the congregations was out in the country among the dairy farms. The other was eight miles away, on Main Street. The village had fifteen hundred residents and most everyone was related one way or another, particularly those souls in the two yoked congregations.

Both churches were old and established, and attended by community leaders. The country-church building was surrounded by a graveyard. The town-church building sat on a large corner lot of mature oaks and maples just on the southern edge of town. It was classic New England style with white wood siding, a set of three tall, clear, glass-paned windows on each side, and a copper-clad steeple with a bell we rang on Sunday mornings. The bell was tolled each Good Friday and pealed each Easter.

We had dinner with the search-committee members from the parish, and it was a warm time of fellowship. It seemed apparent there were no major hurdles, but doing due diligence, the committee sat us down at a large dining room table the next morning and spent a couple hours probing us with questions. They were good questions and we were thankful to see the sincere Christian faith of these men and women the church had entrusted with finding their next pastor.

Finally, done with their questions, they turned to us and said it was our turn.

I asked, "Are you willing to say no to unbelieving parents who request the baptism of their newborn child?"

They responded confidently, "Yes."

"Wait a minute," I said, "let's say the baby whose baptism is being requested is the first grandchild of the town patriarch who's a member of the church, and it's not the baby's father and mother making the request, but the grandfather. He gets his way in most things in his family, the church, and the town. His son—the father of the baby—makes no profession of faith, nor does his son's wife—the baby's mother. But they want to humor grandpa and are willing for him to set things up for the baptism. So now, again, are you willing to say no to that baptism?"

This time there was a significant pause. Then the taciturn dairy farmer sitting at the head of the table chairing the committee spoke: "Yes, we understand it won't be easy, but I think we're ready."

Smiling and relieved, I looked at the chairman and other members and said, "That's all. No more questions."

Shortly thereafter I was ordained and we took up the call to serve First Presbyterian Church and Rosedale Presbyterian Church. Within six months a request came for an infant baptism eerily similar to what I had described. With joy I report that the committee chairman was loving but firm in his support for declining the baptism of this little one born to unbelieving parents, and this despite the important fact that he stood to suffer more alienation and hostility from those told no than any other member of the congregations. It wasn't a nice note to begin on, but then again maybe it was the perfect note for our beginning. We all got through it, and God was gracious to build and reform those churches under this man's and other godly elders' leadership.

Many stories of God's grace could be told here about the faith of those elders through the years, but stories should have a point and we haven't made one yet.

Don't miss the forest for the trees. Our point is not to argue for a certain polity, nor is it to parade the practice of infant baptism. It was something very important I was trying to find out. I wanted to know whether the elders of these churches were prepared to have a pastor who would call them to be faithful in the practice of church discipline.

That's what elders are doing when they withhold baptism or Lord's Table fellowship. This is the practice of church discipline at its most conflictual level. Hearing them state their willingness to take such steps, I had hope of working with elders who would fear God rather than man as they guarded the reputation of our Lord Jesus and the safety of His flock.

So again, do you believe in church discipline? Take a moment and think carefully about it.

Now let's turn to a working definition of "church discipline."

Defining Church Discipline

"Discipline" comes from the word "disciple," so discipline is the work of discipleship. *Merriam-Webster* explains the origin of the word:

> *Discipline* comes from *discipulus*, the Latin word for *pupil*, which also provided the source of the word *disciple* (albeit by way of a Late Latin sense-shift to "a follower of Jesus Christ in his lifetime"). Given that several meanings of *discipline* deal with study, governing one's behavior, and instruction, one might assume that the word's first meaning in English had to do with education.[1]

Close to the time of His ascent, our Lord commanded His disciples to "make disciples of all the nations, . . . teaching them to observe all that I commanded you."[2]

Informal Discipline

There is a chronic misunderstanding of the nature of church discipline today. Most think it refers to formal process only, and typically they mean only formal process that concludes with excommunication. So when someone asks if we believe in church discipline and we answer yes, what we usually mean is that we believe there should be times when the elders of a congregation take the extraordinary step of barring someone from the fellowship of the Lord's Table.

There are times when a man or woman holding membership in the congregation has a conscience and heart so hardened and deceived by sin that he won't listen to the elders' tender appeals or firm admonitions and warnings. In such cases, they must take the formal steps outlined in the church's constitution or bylaws to remove him from the fellowship.

But actually, this is the tiniest part of church discipline, and using these

---

1. *Merriam-Webster*, s.v. "discipline," accessed February 28, 2020, https://www.merriam-webster .com/dictionary/discipline#note-1.
2. Matthew 28:19, 20.

words "church discipline" in this very limited way serves the purpose of hiding all sorts of responsibilities incumbent upon the officers of the church which help prevent their sheep and flock from such a sad moment.

Hypocrisy in Discipline

Think about it this way. The man whose eldest son spends years refusing to obey his father, speaking disrespectfully to his mother, bullying his younger brother, smoking dope in the bathroom, viewing naked flesh on his smartphone, and staying out late every night; that man might tell anyone who asked that, yes, he believes in fathers disciplining their children.

Then, one evening when his son's rebellion is particularly egregious and the father has had a bad day at work, that father might lose it and kick his son out of the house. At which point he has supposedly confirmed his belief in fathers disciplining their children.

But of course, the one thing we certainly know about that father is that he doesn't believe in fathers disciplining their children. He's spent years avoiding the discipline of his son. His excommunicating his son from the household must not be dignified with the word "discipline." Discipline is what this father absolutely refused to do right to the very end when he removed his son. He didn't kick his son out of the house as one tool in his discipleship toolbox. He didn't kick his son out in order to disciple him. He kicked his son out in order to rid himself and his household of the nasty presence of this child his father had raised to be what he had now become.

Back to the church. Elders who refuse to love and teach and correct and encourage and admonish and teach and correct and love and command and exhort and pray for their sheep ought not to be allowed to say they believe in church discipline just because they excommunicated their town's ax murderer after he was caught, tried, and sentenced to life imprisonment. The elder who doesn't love and care for the sheep of his congregation week in, week out, year after year, decade after decade, is absolutely opposed to church discipline.

Don't let him say otherwise.

When Scripture commands God's people to "obey your leaders and submit to them, for they keep watch over your souls as those who will give an account,"[3] elders learn the constant weight of the innumerable incidental responsibilities of their office. What's being commanded here is not submission to excommunication, although that too would be included. Rather, what's being commanded is a posture toward the elders of the church. A disposition. A respectful deference that God here reveals should be the norm between the church's sheep and their shepherds.

Obey your elders. Submit to your elders.

Why?

Because they keep watch over your soul, knowing one day soon they will answer to God for how they did their work. Which souls were saved? Which souls were lost? They will have to give an accounting to their heavenly Father similar to the accounting Jesus gave His Father while praying just prior to His crucifixion:

> While I was with them, I was keeping them in Your name which You have given Me; and I guarded them and not one of them perished but the son of perdition, so that the Scripture would be fulfilled.[4]

By that metric, really much of this whole book is an instruction manual on church discipline.

Preaching and Teaching

Preaching is one of the central methods of making disciples of Jesus, so preaching is at the center of all church discipline. This is why weak preaching, that speaks lots about faith and little about God's law and repentance, bears the fruit of a congregation that has no respect for their elders, neither obeying nor submitting to them. Or rather, a congregation that considers such submission and obedience to elders to be abusive nonsense.

Sheep whose main fare from the pulpit has failed to build them up in the fear of God will show no deference to His servants, the elders.

Yes, preaching is church discipline, and so is teaching. What kind of teaching? Just the formal kind that happens on Sunday mornings and during the midweek family night?

3. Hebrews 13:17.
4. John 17:12.

No, but rather all the teaching—both formal and informal. A healthy elders board will do most of their teaching informally during home fellowship groups, getting together for coffee, men's retreats, talking in the sanctuary and foyer after worship while the children are outside playing... A pastor friend recently said, "The real work of the pastorate and eldership is in casual situations. The sheep, following the lead of the shepherds, are willing to recognize the authority of their shepherd from the pulpit, but not so much over the kitchen table."[5]

In our church, we recently asked the elders if more of them would please change from the first to the second service so there would be shepherds among the second service's sheep, teaching and exhorting and encouraging them.

May I recommend you not spend Sundays before and after worship with your friends or relatives? This is precious time for you to give your full attention to your sheep, diagnosing their needs and helping them carry their burdens. You have the rest of the week for your wife and children, and friendship. Don't waste entire-flock time on blood-family responsibilities that can be put off to later in the day or week. On the other hand, only follow this advice if your wife and children (and friends) know your voice and follow you the rest of the week. You don't ever want to send the message to your own precious children that church members are more important than *they* are. If that's the problem you face, by all means turn and give attention to the sheep of your own household.

One other word of advice. Don't make a federal case out of all your instruction of your sheep, whether at home or at church. If you have something to say, say it and then leave it be. This from the man (Tim) you now know, if you're still reading this book, makes a habit of sewing the point on with an iron thread. In other words, don't assume your sheep are as thick-headed and resistant to instruction as you are. The wise only need a word, and thus the origin of that expression, "a word to the wise."

Many of the most important things we say to our sheep each Lord's Day are said in the door of the church where pastors greet people as they're leaving. A word fitly spoken. Doorways are actually quite private places

---

5. Pastor Andrew Dionne, in conversation.

because people are focused on getting through them—not what's being said between them. So again, don't despise incidental contacts and moments. They can be a crucial part of your discipleship—which is to say, your discipline—of your sheep.

But not just in church and as people are leaving; churches should have home fellowship groups and men's and women's Bible studies and book groups and prayer times, all of which provide many informal times to get to know your sheep and give them a word fitly spoken. Where such times are limited, elders would do well to establish annual home visitations where they go out evenings to visit with their singles and families, asking them some tactful diagnostic questions, probing for fears and pains, asking if there's something they can to do help them, reading a short Scripture, and asking for God's blessing on the house and individual or family members before they say good night and depart. It's all love. It's all good. Done from loving concern, it will all be appreciated. In other words, elder visitations should never be pro forma, because pro forma is cold and reserved and won't be appreciated. It's duty without love.

Formal Discipline

Now that we understand the constancy and incidental nature of your work of church discipline, let's ramp back up to formal discipline. Here are a few things we need to keep in mind concerning formal process, trials, censures, suspension from the Lord's Table, and excommunication.

A Messy Business

Usually the pastors and elders have already invested hundreds of hours working with a sheep, personally, before his name is finally brought up in an elders meeting for consideration of formal discipline.

Say it's a husband and father who's been viewing pornography on his computer. His wife or one of his children discovered it on the family computer and came themselves to an elder after asking the father to, and he refused. Now, for a number of months this man has been in an accountability group and sporadically attending additional weekly or biweekly meetings with one or two elders.

The family is not healthy spiritually. The wife looks depressed and has a bad temper as she mothers her children. She freely admits it and says she's getting bitter. She knows her husband is continuing to use pornography, although he's being more careful to hide it now. She and her husband rarely are intimate, and the husband reports he doesn't find his wife attractive anymore. She may have put on weight after bearing his child, and that's his excuse. She may have a headache every night.

Regardless of the presenting issues in their marriage, when the husband attends his accountability meetings, it's rare for him to report anything more than one week of purity, so the elders who have been working with him have decided it's time to present him to the full session for consideration of a trial and, if he remains unrepentant, suspension from Lord's Table fellowship. He continues in his sin and also continues to partake of communion. As he sees it, "What's the problem? I'm not committing adultery, am I?"

The children are a problem in their school and at church. Their teenagers are hardening in their hearts—the pastor can see it as he preaches and afterwards when he tries to greet them.

The wives of the elders have also been working with his wife, and they too think something formal needs to be done. One of the children just announced she's gay, and there's now talk of separation or divorce. Sounds straightforward, doesn't it?

But the thing is, this man is rich and continues to support the church faithfully. His wife says he's starting to talk about leaving the church for a megachurch across town, and the family's teenagers are all for it and already attend that church's youth groups every now and then. Last summer they went on that church's high school mission trip, and one of the daughters is dating the son of the church's lead pastor.

In other words, whether or not anyone has said it outright during the session meeting, as they sit there in silence, every session member is aware that initiating formal discipline is likely to result in the family leaving the church and proceeding to slander them for harsh treatment and lack of love and grace in their care for the parents and their children. And about the marriage and lust: how is formal discipline going to help if informal discipline hasn't? How is suspension from Lord's Table fellowship going to help if the husband refuses to show up for the trial or to honor his suspension, simply leaving the church instead?

The discussion has been going on for an hour or more when one of the elders who's been working with him says, "I move we charge John Doe with persistent and unrepentant violation of the Seventh Commandment." The other elder who's been working with the man seconds the motion, at which point the pastor serving as moderator asks if there's any debate over the motion. Silence ensues. Pregnant silence. Everyone knows what they're facing, and no one wants to say anything.

Then Doubting Thomas speaks up and says what most of the men are thinking: "What's the use of a trial when we know it's only going to make things worse?"

First, note the declaration that formal discipline will not produce the fruit God ordained.

"God ordained"? Where do we get that from?

We get it from His command. Jesus says,

> If your brother sins, go and show him his fault in private; if he listens to you, you have won your brother. But if he does not listen to you, take one or two more with you, so that by the mouth of two or three witnesses every fact may be confirmed. If he refuses to listen to them, tell it to the church; and if he refuses to listen even to the church, let him be to you as a Gentile and a tax collector.

Then, immediately, Jesus follows the command with promises:

> Truly I say to you, whatever you bind on earth shall have been bound in heaven; and whatever you loose on earth shall have been loosed in heaven.
>
> Again I say to you, that if two of you agree on earth about anything that they may ask, it shall be done for them by My Father who is in heaven. For where two or three have gathered together in My name, I am there in their midst.[6]

The elders have already obeyed the first two commands. Will they

---

6. Matthew 18:15–20.

follow through with the third? Will they tell it to the church by putting this man on trial before the elders?

"But," the reader might respond, "summoning the man before the elders board is not telling it to the church. The session isn't the church."

Actually, it is. Remember chapter 2 on the history of elders in Scripture? There we learned that the elders of Israel were the people's representatives, and so it is in the church today also. There are times when the sin is public, and matters must be dealt with in front of the members of the church, but when the sin is private (as it is in this case), it's appropriate for the trial and censure to also be private. As the elders act, they are the church. The people of God elected them as their representatives.

So, will the elders obey Jesus' command by trying this man for his sin?

Furthermore, will the elders believe the Lord's promise that He will be in the midst of them as they act in His name? Jesus actually promises that God will "bind" and it will be "done for them."

One of the most frequent temptations in elders meetings is utilitarianism. This error is particularly common when the elders are contemplating formal discipline. Thoughts run through everyone's head that constitute the weighing of what positive and negative effects are likely, given this or that action. The premise behind these thoughts is usually that what's right should be determined by which action is likely to produce the greatest good or happiness for the greatest number of people.

If we suspend this man from Lord's Table fellowship, he and his family will leave, and that will be bad. He'll stop giving to the church and all of us will have to give more. Friends of the family in the church will be angry with us. More of our high schoolers will want to go to the megachurch's youth group now that some of their friends are there permanently. The megachurch's pastors will likely have us slandered to them and think worse of us than they already do. We'll get a bad reputation in our city. And all of this for what? For the sake of our consciences—that we can reassure ourselves that we did something?

This isn't even to bring up the threat of a lawsuit. We live in a litigious culture, and it's common for those placed under formal church discipline to threaten to take the elders to civil court over how they claim they were mistreated; or even to the higher court of the church's denomination for some supposed failure to follow the bylaws, the constitution, or the book of church order. It may be unlikely in this particular case, but the threat of litigation hangs over every formal act of church discipline today, whether or not it is spoken audibly during the session meeting.

The Purposes of Formal Church Discipline

It's time to return to our question at the beginning of the chapter: Do we believe in church discipline? Do we believe God has ordained this tool for our use in defending and protecting His sheep and flock? Do we believe God will honor the promises He attaches to this tool which He has ordained?

Maybe the real problem with our utilitarian cost-benefit analyses on such occasions is not that we are counting the cost, but that our counting the cost is leaving out costs we don't want to think about. Here is where we need to remind ourselves of the purposes of formal church discipline. Then we might be able to do another cost-benefit analysis that is more accurate.

1 Protect the Name of Jesus

In his classic on pastoral care, Pastor Richard Baxter has this to say about the necessity of church discipline:

> Sure I am, if it were well understood how much of the pastoral authority and work consisteth in church guidance [discipline], it would be also discerned, that to be against discipline, is near to being against the ministry; and to be against the ministry is near to being absolutely against the church; and to be against the church, is near to being absolutely against Christ. Blame not the harshness of the inference, till you can avoid [disprove] it, and free yourselves from the charge of it before the Lord.[7]

The first purpose of church discipline is to protect the name of Jesus. Remember the account of the woman nominated for elder who was not married to the man she lived with? Remember how the souls in bars downtown were laughing at the church for not knowing this? Why were they laughing?

---

7. Richard Baxter, *The Reformed Pastor* (1656; Banner of Truth, 1974), 111.

Because they despised the Church and her Master, and they were delighted to have this opportunity to mock the Bride of Christ for her notorious failure to abide by God's moral law. To mock the Bride of Christ is to mock our Lord Himself. Should the elders not protect the name and reputation of our Lord at stake with the virtue and holiness of His Bride?

2 Protect the Flock

The second purpose of formal church discipline is to protect the flock. Scripture warns us against the danger of corruption remaining within the flock:

Do not be deceived: "Bad company corrupts good morals."[8]

A little leaven leavens the whole lump of dough.[9]

The classic account of formal church discipline in the New Testament church is this from the Corinthian church. Please take the time to read it, especially if you are familiar with it. We'll comment at several places in between the paragraphs of the text. It's the fifth chapter of 1 Corinthians, in its entirety:

It is actually reported that there is immorality among you, and immorality of such a kind as does not exist even among the Gentiles, that someone has his father's wife. You have become arrogant and have not mourned instead, so that the one who had done this deed would be removed from your midst. (vv. 1–2)

The sin was notorious: it was being "reported." The sin was sexual perversion of the worst sort: a man was having his father's wife. But, as was typical with the Corinthians, this was no hindrance to their pride. They had no shame. No humility. They were not mourning.

Had they mourned over this heinous sin, the apostle declares they would have excommunicated the man—"removed" him from their "midst."

---

8. 1 Corinthians 15:33.
9. Galatians 5:9.

Clearly, then, the failure to remove him was sin on the part of the church and its officers. The Apostle Paul rebukes them for it, then commands them:

> For I, on my part, though absent in body but present in spirit, have already judged him who has so committed this, as though I were present. In the name of our Lord Jesus, when you are assembled, and I with you in spirit, with the power of our Lord Jesus, I have decided to deliver such a one to Satan for the destruction of his flesh, so that his spirit may be saved in the day of the Lord Jesus. (vv. 3–5)

Here the Apostle Paul rises up to his full apostolic authority. Even though he's still far away from them there in Corinth, he declares that he himself has "already judged" this man, and he commands them to judge him also. He stipulates, "when you are assembled," which means the expulsion is to be done publicly, since the sin has been publicly known. It's been notorious.

> Your boasting is not good. Do you not know that a little leaven leavens the whole lump of dough? Clean out the old leaven so that you may be a new lump, just as you are in fact unleavened. For Christ our Passover also has been sacrificed. Therefore let us celebrate the feast, not with old leaven, nor with the leaven of malice and wickedness, but with the unleavened bread of sincerity and truth. (vv. 6–8)

Here the Apostle Paul returns to the pride of the Corinthians, rebuking them for it. It's a theme in the epistle and a theme here in this fifth chapter. Calvin thought it was the Corinthians' besetting sin of pride that caused the Apostle Paul to bring up the particular sin of incest. Incest is so degraded. It's utterly humiliating, and the Apostle Paul shames them over it once again here in this third paragraph.

Then we read the Apostle Paul bringing up this second purpose of church discipline: "a little leaven leavens the while lump of dough." They are to remove the old leaven of this sin and the one committing it so that they and their congregation can return to the purity and holiness to which they have been called by God. It was for this that Christ our Passover Lamb was sacrificed. We have been bought with His blood and are to present ourselves—which is to say, the Church, His Bride—to Him in unleavened purity and holiness.

> I wrote you in my letter not to associate with immoral people; I did not at all mean with the immoral people of this world, or with the covetous and swindlers, or with idolaters, for then you would have to go out of the world. But actually, I wrote to you not to associate with any so-called brother if he is an immoral person, or covetous, or an idolater, or a reviler, or a drunkard, or a swindler—not even to eat with such a one. For what have I to do with judging outsiders? Do you not judge those who are within the church? But those who are outside, God judges. Remove the wicked man from among yourselves. (vv. 9–13)

It is our habit to make a public show of obeying God (and His servant, Paul) while, in reality, refusing to obey. This was what the Corinthians were doing. The Apostle Paul had written a previous letter in which he told them not to associate with "immoral people." Apparently, this had led to the Corinthians making a show of obedience by avoiding various public associations with immoral pagans, while making no effort to avoid associating with immoral brothers and sisters in Christ.

Isn't that always the way it is with us? We give God the obedience that doesn't cost us much, while refusing to give Him the obedience that costs us a lot. What costs more than refusing to eat and drink and welcome to our church-house an upstanding (and likely rich) member whose father's wife enters with him, on his arm? These were the believers in Corinth.

So the Apostle Paul clarifies what he had meant in his former letter. He was not telling them to avoid associating with the immoral worldlings who made no claim to Christ or holiness. He was telling them to avoid associating with their brothers and sisters in Christ who most certainly did make a claim to Christ and holiness.

Then we have a priceless example of Scripture interpreting Scripture; and not just any Scripture, but one of the most frequently abused Scriptures today.

Jesus said, "Judge not, lest ye be judged," and every wicked woman or man responds, "See, Jesus was all about love and He told us *not* to judge." We can hear the believers in the Corinthian church quoting Jesus in justification of their pride as they sat at the Lord's Table, communing with their brother in Christ whose father's wife was next to him.

"Judge not, lest ye be judged. That's what *Jesus* said! Aren't we a wonderfully diverse church? Look at us sitting here next to this son and his dad's wife, acting as if their relationship is the most normal thing in the world! Even pagans could not find it within themselves to demonstrate such tolerance and equanimity. This sin is not even named among them. Most of them are really hot and bothered about incest, but not us! Judge not, lest ye be judged—that's what *Jesus* said! We love sinners. All of us are sinners. Let him who is without sin among us cast the first stone."

The Apostle Paul dispenses with this canard by declaring that, when he commanded them not to associate with the immoral, he wasn't telling them not to have their hair cut or car repaired by immoral unbelievers.

The apostle then brings his fifth-chapter thrashing of the Corinthians and their officers to a close with these declarations, as well as a command, which forever dispense with every smug Christian, and particularly every smug elder in a session meeting who escapes his duty to judge his own sin and the sins of others in his family and church by self-righteously declaring, "Judge not, lest ye be judged!":

> For what have I to do with judging outsiders? Do you not judge those who are within the church? But those who are outside, God judges. Remove the wicked man from among yourselves.

3 Restore the Sinner

All three purposes of church discipline are here in this passage. First, not even the pagans speak of this sin, which means the name of Christ is being blasphemed. Second, the leaven of incest is corrupting the whole church.

And third?

The church in Corinth is to "deliver such a one to Satan for the destruction of his flesh, so that his spirit may be saved in the day of the Lord Jesus" (v. 5). This phrase "so that" indicates a statement of purpose, and that purpose is the salvation of this brother's soul. He is to be removed from the church so that his discipline might produce the fruit of his soul being saved and him being restored to the church.

In fact, in 2 Corinthians, a later letter to the same church, we have what most take to be an indication that this discipline of excommunication did, in fact, restore the sinner through repentance. There we read,

> Sufficient for such a one is this punishment which was inflicted by the majority, so that on the contrary you should rather forgive and comfort him, otherwise such a one might be overwhelmed by excessive sorrow. Wherefore I urge you to reaffirm your love for him.[10]

One final time, then: Do you believe in church discipline?

We have a habit of thinking of the restoration of the sinner as the first purpose of church discipline. But then, faithlessly, we dismiss this possibility and move on to the next item on our agenda. We must not be so faithless.

God appointed the tool of church discipline: first, to protect the honor of His Son; second, to protect His Son's Bride as a whole from the sinful leaven of the one in her midst; and third, to bear the fruit of the salvation of that one who is sinning.

In that order.

Across our churches we have served, we have seen church discipline protect the honor of Christ. We have seen church discipline guard the flock. And yes, we have also seen sinners restored and their souls saved. We both have seen these things again and again throughout our years of shepherding God's flock. Each of these fruits of church discipline give us joy, but there is a special joy when God miraculously produces fruit of repentance and salvation in a believer we cast out who is later restored to the sheepfold.

Again, what does Jesus say about such joy?

> I tell you that in the same way, there will be more joy in heaven over one sinner who repents than over ninety-nine righteous persons who need no repentance.[11]

10. 2 Corinthians 2:6–8.
11. Luke 15:7.

Let's end this chapter with a story we love very much. Remember the
man who was expelled from one of our churches because he was frequently
seen in the streets being quite drunk? He was a founding member of the
church. He was expelled for causing Christ's honor to be harmed. Guess
what happened afterwards? The church records tell us that he came back to
the church after a while and repented in front of the whole congregation.
He asked to be reinstated as a member. Several years later he was nominated
and elected as an elder, and he served in that office for many years. By the
grace of God, and with the help of the Holy Spirit, discipline had made
him a better man. Now there's a reason to believe in discipline!

◆

Every person is to be in subjection to the governing authorities. For there is no authority except from God, and those which exist are established by God. Therefore whoever resists authority has opposed the ordinance of God; and they who have opposed will receive condemnation upon themselves.

—Romans 13:1–2

PART 3

COMMON
DANGERS

BEFORE WE TURN TO SPECIFIC DANGERS AND SINS
of elders, we remind ourselves of this statement above made by the Spirit
of God.

God has ordained all authority and commands us to submit to it.
Or rather, to *them*. To Chancellor Angela Merkel, Prime Minister Boris
Johnson, President Donald Trump—and in the same way, to the pastors
and elders of our church. (You are a member, and you did promise to submit
to your church authorities when you joined, right?)

To point out the obvious, it was clear to God that all men after the
Fall would be sinners and would abuse their authority. After the Fall, it
could never be otherwise, and Scripture is an exhausting account of the
seemingly endless failures of the authorities recorded in its pages—each of
whom was appointed by God Himself and therefore bore His authority in

the exercise of their office, whether king, judge, husband, father, prophet, pastor, or elder.

The reader may ask, "Elder? Where in Scripture do we find an account of elders abusing their authority?"

It's not an account, but a prophecy given matter-of-factly by the Apostle Paul to the elders of the church of Ephesus:

> I know that after my departure savage wolves will come in among you, not sparing the flock; and from among your own selves men will arise, speaking perverse things, to draw away the disciples after them.[1]

Speaking to the elders, he warns them that the threat to the flock will arise "from among your own selves."

Today it can't be said often enough that the abuse of a thing does not invalidate its proper use.

Some cars are lemons, yet we don't stop buying and driving cars. Some milk has soured, but we don't stop drinking milk. Some apples are wormy and rotten; we don't stop eating apples. Some older brothers are mean to their younger brothers; we don't institute a one-child-per-family policy. Some police plant guns on suspects; we don't outlaw guns or rid society of every law enforcement officer. Some lawyers are honest; we don't fire every law school professor.[2]

God created the office of elder knowing it would be abused and that elders would fail at it. So, as we look at some of the most common abuses and failures, don't allow yourself to turn away from the office or from submission to the men God has put over you within His household of faith.

Never forget that it grieved Jesus to look out over the crowds gathering around him, seeing how "distressed and dispirited" they were. Why?

Our Lord said they were "sheep without a shepherd."[3]

Now then, what are some of the more common dangers and failures among elders?

---

1. Acts 20:29–30.
2. Joke.
3. Matthew 9:36; Mark 6:34.

◆

Woe to you, scribes and Pharisees, hypocrites! For you tithe mint and dill and cummin, and have neglected the weightier provisions of the law: justice and mercy and faithfulness; but these are the things you should have done without neglecting the others.

—*Matthew 23:23*

CHAPTER 10

Administration and Money

THIS FIRST FAILURE IS SO COMMON THAT IT could be said to be the fundamental temptation of every elders board and session. During session meetings, almost all the time and energy is spent on administrative and financial matters, leaving little time or energy for caring for the sheep.

What do we mean by "administrative and financial matters"?

Building use policy. Budget development. Job descriptions. Worship attendance. Monthly financial statements. The pastor's study-leave request. The audit of the church financial books. The drop in Sunday school attendance. What venue to use and whom to invite to speak at the church's family conference. Replacement of the church sign. Hiring a custodian. Income trends. Office hours during the Christmas holidays. Capital reserves and expenditures. Roof repair. Denominational per member askings. Wine or grape juice.

The list is endless, but what's important to notice is the absence of pastoral care. One can argue that many of these subjects have some implication and involve some concern for the flock, but those of us who have spent decades going to monthly session meetings know the drill; and if we know our calling, we have grown very weary of this squandering of the session's time and attention.

Again, most congregations' session meetings are spent discussing and arguing over things only tangential to the care, feeding, and protection of God's sheep. Yet the care, feeding, and protection of His sheep is the center of the elder's calling:

> Be on guard for yourselves and for all the flock, among which the Holy Spirit has made you overseers, to shepherd the church of God which He purchased with His own blood.[1]

> Reprove, rebuke, exhort, with great patience . . .[2]

> Therefore, I exhort the elders among you, . . . shepherd the flock of God among you.[3]

Why do session meetings get spent on income, expenditures, facilities, and schedules, rather than people?

It's easier. Money is simple. People are complicated. Money doesn't talk back. People do. So we focus on money and leave the sheep without shepherds. Without encouragement, exhortation, and admonition.

Without love.

Maybe the reader resents that last statement, "without love," but what else should we call it? If our heavenly Father disciplines those He loves, is it not the same with elders? If we don't discipline our sheep, is this not an indication we don't love them?

We spend our time and energy as elders on the objects of our love. If we love money, we spend our meetings talking about money. If we love our building, we spend our time on the building. If we love power, we spend our time planning how to exert and protect it.

If we love our sheep, we spend our time caring for them. Where our treasure is, there our heart is also.

1. Acts 20:28.
2. 2 Timothy 4:2.
3. 1 Peter 5:1, 2.

Some elders might respond something like, "We have a large congregation and we have to pay attention to money and policies and personnel matters." But of course, money, policies, and personnel matters have never required elders to neglect their sheep.

Likely the response would be a protest such as, "We don't neglect the sheep! We love the sheep. We care for the sheep. We spend a lot of time caring for our sheep!" But there's nothing like metrics to tease out the truth. Think back to the last session meeting and count up the time spent on administrative and financial matters compared to the time spent on pastoral care—which is to say, time spent caring for the sheep. Name by name.

What do we mean when we speak of "caring for the sheep"?

Caring for the Sheep in Elders Meetings

Please be patient with the detailed answer. Despite appearances, we do not wish to be exhaustive, but merely suggestive. Caring for the sheep might include:

• • •

Praying and discussing how to support and counsel a young mother in the church whose husband abandoned her and is now pursuing divorce. She is the innocent party. The session knows this through years of pastoral counseling and personal care given this couple and their children by the pastors and elders. The elders responded to this man's abandonment of his wife by appealing to him individually and personally—several of the pastors and elders did so. The session then called him to appear before them to receive and respond to charges, but he refused to appear, and thus was excommunicated. Now, several years later, this man continues to fight a protracted battle for custody of the couple's children. He is committing perjury through his perpetual lies in the courtroom against his friends, family, and wife. Because of this, the mother and her children are suffering deeply.

• • •

Praying and discussing how to respond to reports concerning the high schoolers of the church, received from their Christian school teachers, as well as the pastor who teaches them Wednesday evenings. The reports are disturbing. The teachers and pastor have said they're concerned about the prevalence of cynicism and pride among these young men and women of the congregation. A number of these young men and women are members of the church, having been raised in it and fed the Word of God from a tender age. Several of the high schoolers are sons and daughters of elders and pastors currently serving the church (and presently in the meeting). The reputation of the church among other families of the school and community is being harmed by the conduct of these children. Attempts by the teachers and pastor to deal with these and other sins have not been fruitful.

· · ·

Praying and discussing how to protect the church's sheep from a man in the congregation who has told a number of others in the congregation that two of the elders should be removed from office because of how they treated his friend. His friend left the church a year ago. Before he left, this friend had been reported to the elders by his teenage son for leaving pictures of naked flesh on the family computer and getting drunk in front of the family. He did both repeatedly. The two elders being accused of abusing this friend had been meeting with him the year before his departure, praying and seeking to help him toward repentance for his sin. Along with a pastor skilled in working with troubled marriages, these elders had counseled with the man and his wife, but as the months went by it became clear the man was not repentant. He continued to violate his marriage vows and the purity of his marriage bed. Finally, he took his wife and children to another church where the pastor was happy to receive them and made no attempt to contact the church they had just left. The man's friend has spent the past year spreading lies about the lack of love on the part of the two elders who had worked with him before he left.

The man still in the congregation is himself taking his friend's lies and spreading them within the church. It's particularly complicated because the wife of the man given to drunkenness and pornography is the longtime Bible Study Fellowship instructor at a neighboring evangelical church. The members of the church have no knowledge of the sins of the departed man, nor of the year these elders and one of the pastors spent giving him—and his wife—kind, loving, and personal pastoral care.

. . .

Praying and discussing how to help a young woman who recently joined the church and is near the end of her freshman year at a local Christian college. Her father is an elder in a conservative church in a city four hours away. Following spring break, this young woman had a nervous breakdown during which she confessed to a pastor's wife that she and her stepfather had a sexual relationship all the way through junior high and high school, and she now fears that her stepfather is grooming her elementary-aged sister. Normally, this would not be discussed by the full elders board, but in this case attempts to speak and work with this man's pastor to expose this father's sin and report the crimes to the civil magistrate were met by the pastor at the father's church having an attorney (also an elder there) write a letter threatening a civil lawsuit against the church and her pastors for defamation of character if the daughter's accusation against her father is ever spoken of again, to anyone. The church is being threatened with litigation and the session must decide how to respond.

. . .

Praying and discussing how to respond to the deacons, who are refusing to purchase a new copier for the church office. The need for the copier was thoroughly presented to the budget committee, who put this expenditure into the year's budget, which the congregation then approved. Given the large expense, the copier was an actual line item in the budget, so the congregation heard about the need and voted to approve that expense. Nevertheless, the deacons are opposing the expenditure each time the administrative assistant requests it, and there is a growing root of bitterness among them that is in the process of corrupting many.

The backstory is that one of the deacons owns a failing office-products store and presented the church a bid on this new copier, but his price and the rating of the brand he sells, along with the cost of the service plan he would provide, were far higher than his competitor. The elders have admonished this man concerning his selfishness and anger in deacons meetings several times in the past two years; he's been a faithful deacon for many years; his wife is deep in Alzheimer's, and he cares for her at home; their daughter is the church treasurer; and so on. Sadly, the younger men on the deacons board are not yet able to stand against this man's anger and hostility, so the poison is spreading in the deacons board.

. . .

Praying and deciding how to bring peace to the women of the congregation who are in the midst of a nasty argument over all things foodie. They argue over on-demand versus scheduled nursing of babies. They argue about gluten. They argue over whether or not sugar should be allowed in dishes brought to weekly home fellowship groups; and if so, whether the children should be allowed to eat that sugar-added food. They argue whether or not honey should be considered sugar. They argue over whether dessert should be offered at potlucks. They argue over the health benefits of raw milk. They argue about which grinder makes the best flour for the best bread. There's one grass-fed-beef group and one grain-fed-beef group, and they spit on each other. There's a cage-free-chicken lobby, and they are quite intense about it. There's a woman who runs a small-scale truck farm who is pressuring all the other women to source their produce locally. A number of the worst offenders are the wives of pastors, deacons, and elders, so it's hard to get consensus on the best approach, since a number of the elders are simply speaking up in defense of their wives (without anyone acknowledging it). Sadly, some of these elders seem to have fallen backwards in their willingness to lead and sanctify their wives recently, so there's that too.

Thinking about the intricacies of this sin dogging the congregation, the pastor (who is moderator) is going cross-eyed and has a headache.

. . .

Now, as we said at the beginning of this chapter, these examples are not exhaustive. They're merely suggestive. Some readers might think a number of the scenarios above are unrealistic, but being older, we know these situations, which require tact, pastoral wisdom, and leadership, are normal to the point of being mundane. If any particular church's elders find that the examples stretch their credulity, we'd respond by wondering if the elders know their sheep and congregation. Almost every church with young families and infants is going to deal with tension among mothers over whether nursing should be on-demand or scheduled. Also conflict between the elders and deacons, the deacons and the church office, the church office and the ushers, janitor, and wedding coordinator. Add COVID-19, social distancing, and face masks to the mixture, and *everyone* begins to see cross-eyed.

So no, these examples are not extraordinary, but ordinary, and it's the session's job to resolve (or help resolve) these conflicts.

Avoiding the Work

Right here, we realize why sessions spend their meetings on administrative and financial matters. It's intimidating to elders to even think about such conflicts, let alone decide the best way to resolve them. Thus we embrace the tyranny of the urgent, which allows us to avoid the larger and more chronic threats to the well-being of the flock.

We have to keep the lights on, so let's talk about our giving trends and the budget deficit.

The church office needs a new copier, the congregation approved a new line item in the budget, so let's send an email to the moderator of the deacons telling him to get it done.

The pastor has done his duty by contacting the pastor of the incestuous father, but he should be quiet about it now. No need to risk litigation. His wife can counsel the daughter as needed, and do we elders really need to hear any more about this? We're not sure it needed to be brought up here in the meeting. Shouldn't this have stayed private?

Readers will notice that, insidiously, what starts as a tendency to concentrate on administrative and financial matters soon becomes a principle the session enforces. How many times have we heard a pastor asking his elders for help with a sensitive matter of pastoral care, only to have one of the elders shut down any possibility of the pastor getting counsel and help with the sheep by declaring quite self-righteously, "Do we really need to know about this? Shouldn't this be a private matter? Can't you just handle it, Pastor ——?"

It's common for elders to refuse to do their pastoral work, covering up their betrayal of their calling by claiming high principles for that betrayal. There are few principles higher in our HIPAA age than confidentiality, and how successful it is in stifling elders work. "We should *not* be talking about this" and "We don't need to know about this" morph into "Pastor, you shouldn't have told us anything about this. We pay *you* to handle these things!"

So rather than the plurality of elders bringing their joint wisdom and prayer before the throne of God in defense and support of the sheep, the pastor is the goat sent out of the session meeting bearing the people's sins. Alone.

How do we correct this habit on display in so many of our churches' session meetings?

Getting Priorities Straight

First, elders (and churches) need to be taught what the Bible says about their office and work. This is rarely done and leads to false expectations concerning the nature of the office and the demands it places on men and their wives and children. This book is an attempt to open up that teaching, and we hope it will be helpful to that end.

Second, pastors and elders who have come to a biblical understanding of the office and work of the shepherds of Christ's Church would do well to develop a deep understanding and sympathy for other elders' fears of their own inadequacy and lack of understanding.

Third, the session's moderator should place a time for devotions and prayer at the beginning of each session meeting. But not just any devotions: he should work to ensure that these times of instruction from Scripture will regularly reinforce the pastoral and spiritual nature of the work of elders. This time in Scripture at the beginning of the meeting should regularly remind every man present of the promise of God through His Holy Spirit to give wisdom to those who ask.

In our session meetings, we rotate the leadership and teaching at the beginning of each meeting between all the pastors and elders, and this is helpful in growing the teaching ability of each of us. On the other hand, as moderator, the pastor should frequently teach during the meeting what he thinks the men need to hear about this or that challenge facing them individually or as a group.

The pastor's most important leadership and instruction is always with his own elders, and he should never be bashful about using the time of session meetings to call the men back to the truths of God's Word. Moderators who don't use this privilege will lose it, not only for themselves, but possibly for all future pastors. Elders need to defend this responsibility of their pastor, not allowing him to be lazy or to shy away from instructing them; nor should they tolerate complaining from their fellow elders about the pastor's efforts to lead in this way. Cultivating and guarding his elders' unity, wisdom, and faith for the work given them by God is the pastor's most important work, and often his greatest challenge. It must be done with deep sensitivity, since these are his peers and they may be even less tolerant of his failures than members of the congregation.

Finally, it's imperative that the session's regular stated meetings have an agenda prepared beforehand which the moderator has gone over, considering carefully the relative priority each item should have and when it should be brought up in the meeting. In other words, don't do the easy things at the beginning of the meeting, only turning to the pastoral care of the divisive man, the incestuous father, and the sins of the pastors' and elders' children at the end of the meeting when everyone's tired and wants to go home to bed. If someone else prepares the agenda, there's still no reason for the moderator not to switch things around so that the elders hit the spiritual care issues early while they're still fresh and have faith for addressing things that are really difficult.

Not that we lord it over your faith, but are workers with you for your joy; for in your faith you are standing firm.

—*2 Corinthians 1:24*

CHAPTER 11

Lording It Over the Sheep

IT MIGHT WELL BE HELPFUL FOR US TO SET A rule over ourselves that this or one of the similar warnings from our Lord be read at the beginning of each of our elders meetings:

Then Jesus spoke to the crowds and to His disciples, saying: "The scribes and the Pharisees have seated themselves in the chair of Moses; therefore all that they tell you, do and observe, but do not do according to their deeds; for they say things and do not do them. They tie up heavy burdens and lay them on men's shoulders, but they themselves are unwilling to move them with so much as a finger. . . . They love the place of honor at banquets and the chief seats in the synagogues, and respectful greetings in the market places, and being called Rabbi by men."[1]

Jesus' warnings here, issued inside the Temple—the very turf of the scribes and Pharisees—continue for another thirty-two verses, but we'll limit ourselves to these first seven verses.

1. Matthew 23:1–4, 6–7.

Note first that His warnings throughout Matthew 23 are given to both "the crowds" and "His disciples." It is not just those who sit in positions of authority who are endangered by hypocritical leaders, but also those they lead. It is the purpose of authority to protect those under them, so when those in authority are abusing that authority, those under them must be warned that their leaders' hypocrisy leaves them exposed and vulnerable.

Seating Themselves

The warnings begin with Jesus declaring that the church leaders of His time had "seated themselves in the chair of Moses." The "chair of Moses" refers to the seventy elders God told Moses to gather to assist him in ruling the sons of Israel:

> Gather for Me seventy men from the elders of Israel, whom you know to be the elders of the people and their officers and bring them to the tent of meeting, and let them take their stand there with you.[2]

Much as the Roman Catholic Church today makes exclusive claims to "apostolic succession," the scribes and Pharisees of Jesus' time claimed they were the rightful successors to Moses' elders. Yet it's apparent from the text above that Moses' seventy had not appointed themselves. Under the direction of God, Moses chose them from those serving as elders among the Israelites. So, again, we see the choice of God through God's servant Moses, as well as the choice of the people from among whom Moses made his choice. Each of the seventy had already been chosen by the people to serve as their elders.

Contrariwise, the scribes and Pharisees had "seated themselves," declares our Lord. They thought they were superior to the people in all things religious, so they put themselves forward as the officers of the church. We might say they ran for office and then rigged the vote. This is the first condemnation of these men given by our Lord.

---

2. Numbers 11:16.

Tying Up Heavy Burdens

Then this terrible judgment that these self-selected, self-appointed church leaders were hypocrites proper. They said one thing and did another. They taught the right and did the wrong.

Not only that, but they taught the right in such a way as to make the right particularly difficult for those they were leading. What they called the people to was not just burdensome, but heavily burdensome. They did not call the people to look to God for grace to fulfill His law. Rather, they loaded the people down with such heavy particularities, which they claimed the law required, that the people were in danger of despair. No Gospel. Just law. This was the main fare fed God's sheep by the church leaders at the time of our Lord.

Yet, it's even worse. Not only was their teaching of God's law burdensome, and heavily so, but after laying their heavy burdens on the sheep, these shepherds refused to help the sheep carry those burdens.

Isaiah prophesied that the Good Shepherd "will gather the lambs and carry them in His bosom; He will gently lead the nursing ewes." "A bruised reed He will not break and a dimly burning wick He will not extinguish."[3] This was not the shepherds of Israel in Jesus' time.

The best boss I ever had was Dan Daly of ServiceMASTER's master franchise in Boston. Along with a friend or two enlisted from seminary, each month we'd go down to clean carpets at the Cabot Corporation headquarters occupying the top five floors in one of Boston's skyscrapers. Dan would meet us at the loading zone in front of the main entrance where his yellow station wagon sat holding the rotary floor-cleaning machines we used for our work.

These machines were quite heavy and very awkward to lift. Plus, they were inside a station wagon, so you had to reach in the back of the wagon and lift them with your back fully extended. It was the hardest task of the day. But none of us young men were ever successful in our attempts to lift them out ourselves. This burdensome task we were getting paid to do was always done by Dan instead. We were in our late twenties and early thirties,

3. Isaiah 40:11; 42:3.

Dan was in his late fifties, and each time we'd try to do it, he'd brush us aside with the words, "Here, let me get that."

This was Dan, and it was the reason we all had such deep affection for him. Honestly, we did try our best to steal the hard work from him, but it was hard to beat him to the hard work or take it away from him without making him mad. He was a leader who believed he should always help his workers bear their burdens. Most of us have had a boss like Dan at some point in our lives, but I'm not sure most of us have had elders and pastors like that.

Dan never lorded it over his employees—just the opposite. He cared for us and served us and helped us carry our loads. Obviously, then, every time I could work for Dan, I jumped at the chance, and I never had any trouble getting other guys at seminary to come along.

The scribes and Pharisees weren't like that. They made difficult loads even heavier, then stood to the side and watched the sheep trying to carry them. They thought to themselves, "We're no beasts of burden. We're important. We can't risk hurting our backs. What would the sheep do without us if we injured ourselves trying to help them?"

Exasperating the Sheep

After this warning and rebuke, our Lord added another condemnation of these church leaders. They "love the place of honor at banquets and the chief seats in the synagogues, and respectful greetings in the market places, and being called Rabbi by men" (v. 6).

At work and on the jobsite and in the warehouse and out in the field and in the break room and on the assembly line, we all have names for bosses like this. Children have names for fathers like this. I'll not list some of those names here, but I will point out that Scripture commands fathers not to "exasperate" their children. And this is one of the most common ways we as fathers do, in fact, exasperate our children. We require our children to honor us in the way they address us in their speech and the places they leave vacant so we can sit there ourselves. We require them to honor us in the obedience they give us, and we delight in making our commands burdensome. Justifying our commands by the need to develop "character" in our sons, we make our commands heavier than they need to be, and then we refrain from helping them with the load we've placed on their shoulders.

My wife told me about a young son in our church whose father was infuriated that the lawn mower wasn't working. He yelled at his son to go out into the yard and fix it, but did nothing to explain the problem or give encouragement. And of course, he did not go outside himself and help his son. Fearful of his father's terrible wrath, the son obeyed his father and went out to see what his twelve-year-old body and mind could accomplish. Meanwhile, his father sat inside and seethed against the lawn mower and his son's constant ineptitude. My wife and I were heartbroken for that son, his brothers and sisters, and his mother (who had recounted the incident to my wife).

The actual command of Scripture to fathers gives a reason for not exasperating our sons and daughters, and that reason is perfectly applicable to pastors and elders who lord it over their sheep: "Fathers, do not exasperate your children, so that they will not lose heart."[4]

Elders too are capable of exasperating their sheep, causing them to lose heart. So what are some examples of elders lording it over their congregations?

Intimacy Required

The most common way it's done in the church today is men treating the office of elder as a sinecure. What is a sinecure?

A sinecure is an office that benefits the man holding it with title, honor, and often money, but requiring of him little or no work. The word is from two Latin words meaning "without" and "care," so a sinecure is a pastor's living or salary that carries with it no expectation that the pastor will actually care for his congregation.

Same with elders: men elected to an office who hold the title of respect, "elder," without any parallel expectation that they will do an elder's work

---

4. Colossians 3:21.

and care for their sheep. They are lords of the manor presiding over a bunch of flunkies who clean the carriages, carry and empty the slop buckets, cook and serve the meals, wash the clothes, plant and weed and harvest the crops, keep up the gardens, wash the floors, raise their children, provide emotional companionship for their wife, and do it all in such a way as to turn enough of a profit on the land so that the lord's lording it over them can continue and be passed down to his eldest son.

This may be the way of aristocracy, but it's not the way of any good shepherd in the Church of Jesus Christ.

Rather, Jesus commands those of us called to serve His sheep as pastors and elders with these words:

> You know that those who are recognized as rulers of the Gentiles lord it over them; and their great men exercise authority over them. But it is not this way among you, but whoever wishes to become great among you shall be your servant; and whoever wishes to be first among you shall be slave of all. For even the Son of Man did not come to be served, but to serve, and to give His life a ransom for many.[5]

Elders are not to teach and command the flock without knowing their sheep personally. How can their teaching and commanding be any good when they don't know their flock? Every good dairyman gives personal care to his cows based on the cow's infections, the butterfat content of her milk, whether she casts her calves, and so on.

How can we choose our Scripture texts for teaching our Sunday school classes without knowing the condition of this man's marriage, without knowing that this mother has her children in daycare, without knowing that that timid soul is endlessly fearful of God's wrath and never takes communion . . .

Yes, as we've pointed out repeatedly in this book, knowing our sheep requires intimacy, and intimacy carries many risks. Intimacy with sheep requires getting in the sheepfold with them, and if you do that you'll begin to smell like them.

5. Mark 10:42–45.

Nevertheless, our Lord commands us,

Do not be called leaders; for One is your Leader, that is, Christ. But the greatest among you shall be your servant. Whoever exalts himself shall be humbled; and whoever humbles himself shall be exalted.[6]

Bishop J. C. Ryle comments on these hard words of rebuke of the church leaders of Jesus' time recorded throughout Matthew 23, which

contains the last words which the Lord Jesus ever spoke within the walls of the temple. Those last words consist of a withering exposure of the scribes and Pharisees, and a sharp rebuke of their doctrines and practices. Knowing full well that His time on earth was drawing to a close, our Lord no longer keeps back his opinion of the leading teachers of the Jews. Knowing that he would soon leave his followers alone, like sheep among wolves, he warns them plainly against the false shepherds by whom they were surrounded.[7]

One last Scripture to motivate us to love our sheep:

So when He had washed their feet, and taken His garments and reclined at the table again, He said to them, "Do you know what I have done to you? You call Me Teacher and Lord; and you are right, for so I am. If I then, the Lord and the Teacher, washed your feet, you also ought to wash one another's feet. For I gave you an example that you also should do as I did to you. Truly, truly, I say to you, a slave is not greater than his master, nor is one who is sent greater than the one who sent him. If you know these things, you are blessed if you do them.[8]

Embrace it. Get your sheep's smell on you. Humble yourself and love them as Jesus loved His twelve and loves you and me still.

6. Matthew 23:10–12.
7. J. C. Ryle, comments on Matthew 23:1–12, *Expository Thoughts on the Matthew* (1856; Banner of Truth, 2012), 238.
8. John 13:12–17.

And there arose also a dispute among them as to which one of them was regarded to be greatest.

—*Luke 22:24*

CHAPTER 12

Conflict in the Session

I N CHAPTER 6, WE EXPLAINED THE NECESSITY
of elders and pastors engaging in conflict in order to protect the
peace and purity of the Church. This is one of the reasons God calls
men—not women—to the office. Mothers and children should be protected. Mothers shouldn't have to protect their household from attack. It's
the father's job, and pastors and elders are the fathers of the household of
faith, the Church of the Living God.

Conflict is part of their job description. As Matthew Henry points out,
"The way to preserve the peace of the church is to preserve the purity of it."[1]

We also explained earlier that there is good conflict and bad conflict.
This chapter further addresses the question of how to tell the difference,
with some suggested ways the session can work to keep the session's own
conflict good.

Bad conflict within the session can corrupt the work of the elders, and
thereby the well-being of the congregation. It is the worst thing possible

1. Comments on Leviticus 24:10–23, *Commentary on the Whole Bible*, 142.

when those who should be peacemakers themselves get in a fight with each other and take their eyes off the flock, and this partly because the flock never take their eyes off their shepherds. Rather, they watch them and learn. If Papa and Mama are fighting, the children fight too, and it's the same in the church. If the session is fighting, the flock will fight. It's inevitable. Bad conflict is contagious in any organization, and it's particularly destructive when it flows from the top to the bottom.

The elders cannot bring peace and unity to a congregation while they are at war amongst themselves. And yet, we've said they must engage in conflict. So how do we distinguish between healthy session conflict and session conflict that is destructive to the purity and peace of the church?

5 Marks of a Healthy Session

We think the most helpful way to answer this question will be to identify distinguishing marks of healthy sessions, especially as they relate to how sessions deal with conflict.

1 The healthy session argues.

First, the healthy session doesn't quarrel. They argue. What's the difference?

When we quarrel, it's our own pride and power we are defending. We're not seeking the common good, but pursuing our own personal gain.

Because they love each other, the healthy session doesn't quarrel. The Spirit of God has given them a common affection and mutual self-interest. One man guards another man's feelings. So there are times in the midst of the debate that one elder opposing the argument being made by another will stop and perfect the other elder's argument in order to make his brother's case stronger. This is not necessarily because he's become convinced the other man's right, but because what's being pursued in the debate is wisdom and truth, and the best way to get at wisdom and truth is by making the debate as perceptive and revelatory as possible.

Remember, good conflict is a way of discovering truth. Good conflict involves arguments about issues. True, the debate can go on for a long time and sometimes become heated, but it is always focused on the issue at hand.

Bad conflict, by contrast, involves power struggles. It is not about finding truth through considering all aspects of an issue. Rather, it is about who wins and who gets to dictate what the others do. In good conflict, a man sticks to a principle until he is convinced by the others that something is wrong with it. In bad conflict, a man has no principles except this: he must get his way, and the others must do as he likes.

2 *The healthy session's members all participate.*

Second, the healthy session has each man join in the debate. There aren't one or two men who refuse to speak or take sides because they are waiting until the debate is exhausted, at which point they rise to declare the truth of the matter.

When the hard work of debate is being done by the others, staying above the fray is not manly. God has placed each man on the board, and each man should join in the hurly-burly, trusting God that he has thoughts that matter and that he should contribute to the deliberation, and thus the session's final judgment.

The healthy session has faith in the fruit of the debate and attributes that fruit to the work of the Holy Spirit—not just at the end, but during and through the debate. The elders of the church in Antioch had much debate over the circumcision of Gentile believers, and they could not resolve the debate themselves, so wisdom led them to send their argument down to the church of Jerusalem to be resolved there. The church and her officers there in Jerusalem during what we refer to as the "Jerusalem Council" did the hard work of much more debate until, finally, they came to a resolution.

The whole account is instructive for how to resolve divisions and restore peace in the church, but what's noteworthy for our purposes here is how the apostles and elders spoke of their extended argument when they announced the resolution. They wrote their resolution in a letter to the church in Antioch, prefacing the specifics of that resolution with this phrase declaring the nature of the process that had produced it, which, we note, included "much debate" (v. 7): "For it seemed good to the Holy Spirit and to us . . ." (v. 28). This shows the apostles and elders of the Jerusalem church had faith that God was working in and through their arguments, and that's the faith every elder must bring into each session meeting. Every meeting begins with prayer for God's wisdom as the members of session deliberate, so no man should consider himself superior to the process of deliberation.

Some men will not feel free to join in the debate, not because they refuse to sully themselves with the hurly-burly, but because they are younger than the others, shy, or intimidated. These men need to be pulled out of themselves with gentleness and understanding over time, but do not mistake the proud man's silence for the humble man's lack of confidence or timidity. Do not deal with the proud man gently if he consistently waits until the end to speak, and then speaks ex cathedra. Such a man needs to be admonished to lower himself to being argued with and contradicted by his brothers in Christ. Assure him, privately, that this hurly-burly is not a failure, but a success, and that he should join in so that he is humbled and can, in the end, take joy in the fruit the Holy Spirit produces from their hard work.

3 The healthy session recognizes a diversity of gifts.

Third, the healthy session is not impatient with the outliers in their midst, but recognizes and honors the diversity of gifts which God has put in their midst, and which is necessary for their work. The healthy session cultivates and protects that diversity.

Often there are men on the session whom it's easy to grow impatient with because their contributions regularly put a damper on where the group as a whole finds itself heading naturally. Take the man with the gift of mercy, for instance. It is often the case that most of the session is ready to resolve an issue or discipline a man long before the elder with the gift of mercy is on board. It can be frustrating to see all the elders ready to act resolutely on a difficult matter, then listen as the man of mercy cautions the board, suggesting there may be more charitable ways of viewing an issue or an individual's behavior than have been proposed by anyone else on the board.

We have had a number of men like this on our sessions, and it's easy to listen to their contributions with impatience, and then to dismiss their hesitancy and proceed to the resolution everyone else seems to feel is needed right now. But if we do so, we should realize we may very well be silencing or quenching the Holy Spirit's work among us.

In this connection, here's wise counsel, again from Calvin's dear brother in ministry, Martin Bucer, pastor of the newly reformed church in Strasbourg:

> To one he gives the skill of teaching clearly and understandably, while not endowing him with so much grace in exhorting; to another he gives ability to exhort warmly and seriously, without also enabling him to be powerful in the teaching and exposition of the scriptures. To another he grants an especially effective enthusiasm in chastising and disciplining, though he may not be able to achieve much in either teaching or exhorting. One the Lord has endowed with a fine upright and honest spirit to care for the whole congregation and to provide timely provision and protection where Satan wants to break in, while he does not have great abilities otherwise, either in teaching or exhorting. There are those whom the Lord has appointed to exercise their ministry conscientiously and usefully to the bruised and wounded, warmly and powerfully comforting them and applying the right measure of gravity and discipline, but who are not particularly effective in other aspects of the pastoral office.
>
> Therefore, since the pastoral office involves such a great and important work, and one which so long as we live here is unending, that of presenting the church of Christ in all its members without fault, without stain or wrinkle, this office requires many sorts of ministry and work.[2]

The healthy session will work to honor, and not be dismissive of, these individual gifts spread out among its elders. The one gifted at teaching, but not exhorting. The one gifted at exhorting, but not teaching. The one who's a natural at admonishing and correcting, but neither teaching nor exhorting. The one gifted at watching over and protecting the flock from the wiles of Satan. The one who has the gift of compassion and mercy, and thus is particularly good at gently leading and disciplining the weak and timid of the flock.

This is so helpful. Many of us are tempted to think our particular gifts are the most important ones, abusing our gifts by running over the other

2. Bucer, 34.

gifts God has given other men on the session. Others of us are tempted to think our particular gifts are of lesser significance, and we should just be quiet and let the strong and loud men lead as they wish. Of course, pride is the besetting sin of the former, and jealousy and bitterness of the latter.

Let us suggest you read this quote above from Bucer aloud to your fellow elders and commit yourselves to honor and promote each man's gifts. This not in order to make each man feel like he has a reason to serve as an elder (although that is also important), but rather to exhort the timid and compassionate men to bring their gifts to bear on the work of the elders, knowing that God has placed them and their gifts on the session because there is a great diversity of needs in the flock.

4 The healthy session spends time in fellowship and prayer.

Fourth, the healthy session spends time in fellowship and prayer. We've noticed the debate over difficult things and the resolution of that debate within our sessions often is as much a function of the degree of affection and trust we have for one another as it is a function of the relative intractability of the issue before us. We might state the matter this way: often, there is an inverse correlation between length of time it takes to debate and decide a matter and the degree of warmth and trust that is present among the members of session. Less warmth and trust results in more time debating and deciding. More warmth and trust results in less time debating and deciding.

As moderators, we should have some idea which issues on the agenda will be difficult, so we carve out a large amount of time for them and try to get to them as soon as possible in the meeting. This is wise, as far as it goes. But there's another way to address the difficulty of the discussion beyond where it is on the agenda and how much time is designated for it.

Start your meeting with devotions and prayer. Start your meeting reminding yourselves that you are doing the work of God and may count on God's help as you care for the sheep bought with the precious blood of His Son. And if these weren't the particular themes of the devotions given at the beginning of the meeting, stop the meeting for a few minutes (or ask the moderator to do so), and read one of the many promises of Scripture concerning your work; then pray and move back to the work.

The session's work of debate and conflict over doctrinal matters or schism is extremely difficult. Don't minimize that difficulty. Rather, plead with God to help you. Nothing is too difficult for Him, and again and again you will learn that He answers prayer and shows a way to restore the peace and purity of the flock—a way that would never have occurred to you personally. It's a wonderful realization!

One final suggestion here. If the meeting's tone is particularly tense as you come together—whether that tension is due to the various life circumstances of individual members of the session or the difficult agenda items everyone knows will have to be addressed—take half an hour at the beginning of the meeting following devotions to have the men you know are most in need of encouragement and prayer share with the others what is going on in their lives. Sometimes it's best to go around the entire group and have each pastor and elder share, stopping after each and having the man next to him pray for him. Sometimes it's best to pick out the men you know are most in need. Half an hour to an hour is usually the time taken up with this bearing of each other's burdens, but this is not time wasted.

This too is the work of the session, and if you don't take time for it, you'll spend that time elsewhere before the session meeting is over. In fact, it's frequently the case that whatever time is given at the beginning of the session meeting to bearing one another's burdens is equal to, or even less, than the time you would have taken bickering and fighting over an issue, had you not become unified through personal sharing and prayer at the beginning.

5 *The healthy session's members like each other.*

Fifth, the healthy session stands around and talks at the end of the meeting, and this regardless of how late the meeting adjourns. Why?

Because session members of the healthy session actually like each other.

This mark of the healthy session is not prescriptive, but descriptive. Diagnostic. Do you stand around and love and talk with each other after the meeting? If not, then you need to spend time building fellowship and love among yourselves. Even if you prefer short meetings and getting back home as soon as possible, you should realize it's unlikely for a session that doesn't enjoy each other to have a congregation that *does* enjoy each other. Like shepherds, like sheep.

Cultivate and grow in your love for your pastors and fellow elders so that your congregation will cultivate and grow in their love for their shepherds and one another. For one thing, it's much easier for shepherds to lead sheep who love them. For another, Jesus said the world would know we are Christians by observing our love for one another, and every household's love rises no higher than the love of their father for their mother, and both father and mother for their children.

Mutual Respect between Pastors and Elders

There remains one aspect of the work of restoring and guarding the peace and purity of the flock that must be addressed, and this is the relationship between the session and its pastor.

In a healthy session, the elders respect the pastor for his good leadership. The elders do not respect him because he has a title or an academic degree. They respect him because he works hard for the benefit of the church and sacrifices time and effort to care for the souls of the sheep and the elders. They respect him because he submits to what the session decides, even if it goes against his own wishes. They respect him because he comes to the session well prepared and leads the session well. One of a moderator's most important tasks is to recognize bad conflict and keep it from poisoning the session. Instead, he should stimulate good conflict so that the session meetings produce righteous results. A good leader knows his elders and anticipates when and why good conflict may turn into bad conflict.

In a healthy session, the pastor respects the elders for their hard work. He does not respect the elders because they have money, because they have hired him, because they could fire him, or because they have been in office forever. He respects them because they have the trust of the flock. He respects them because they devote time and effort to do the work of elders, and do it well. He respects them because they are willing to engage in good conflict. He respects them because they submit to his good leadership.

The principles of good leadership are the same in every organization, be it an elders board or the board of a business or public institution. Good leaders are consistent and transparent. Good leaders know the difference between good and bad conflict, and they promote the first while fending off the second. Good leaders do not discuss matters with individual elders before or after a session meeting except when necessary to squelch bad conflict. Good leaders begin a session meeting with a pre-announced agenda, and they stick to it. Go read a management guide. It is all the same.

Clearly, then, the relationship between the session and the pastor is a delicate balance of mutual submission and recognition of authority. Maintaining this balance is not easy. It requires the investment of a lot of time, not just in lengthy session meetings, but also in time spent in fellowship. A healthy session can be recognized by the fact that the elders and the pastor and their families go on retreats together and enjoy spending time together in prayer, devotions, and—importantly—play. Both pastors and elders must make conscious efforts to build relationships of mutual trust and love, and we can't do this if we never spend time together outside session meetings.

Many things can go wrong in the relationship between the elders and the pastor. Both of us have worked with sessions that included one or two elders addicted to power. One elder in one of our churches always came to session meetings unprepared. He would listen to the pastor for a while and then oppose him no matter what the issue was. One of his favorite phrases was, "Pastor, why don't you come up with a solution?" And when the pastor made a proposal, he would respond, "This does not work in our church. Why don't you come up with something?" He would favor one thing at one session meeting and the opposite at the next, always blaming the pastor for his inability to come up with something. Once he told the pastor, "We elders are the bosses of this church because we bring the money. Pastors are mere employees taking orders from us." Session meetings were unproductive because they were all wasted on bad conflict.

Sadly, his fellow elders never called him to order; one was his wife, and the other an old buddy of his. Weak elders like that man do not tolerate good elders at their side. They drive them away. In fact, that church had a pattern of elders leaving office and the church after one term. Over time, the sheep had resigned themselves to that vicious situation. Can you guess why?

Because that elder had money.

Sadly, no pastor had ever confronted the man. Should we be surprised? Weak elders like that hire weak pastors they know they can control; they hire soft men who won't stand up and fight for the well-being of the flock.

It's not surprising that this situation continued while the church dwindled down in membership and worship attendance.

Can a situation like this be rescued? Yes, and with the help of God it has been. But it takes a lot of stamina on the part of the pastor. When one of us was called to be the pastor of that church, it was (as the power-hungry elder confessed later) by accident. Once this elder realized the new pastor would oppose his control over the session and the church, he engaged in a dirty fight for power. But eventually, he resigned and left the church—not without slander and accusations against the pastor. It was a tough fight. But it was worth it, for that church, by the grace of God, began to grow again and learned to enjoy the sweet fellowship of the people of God.

What's the lesson?

One weak elder makes all the difference. A culture of weak elders and weak pastors can destroy a church. Therefore, dear elder, pay attention to what the Apostle Paul said to the Ephesian elders: "Pay careful attention to yourselves."[3] Watch out for men who lust for power and desire to become elders. If you do not oppose them, they may destroy the flock.

3. Acts 20:28 (ESV).

For the Son of Man is going to come in the glory of His Father with His angels, and will then repay every man according to his deeds.

—*Matthew 16:27*

PART 4

LAST
THINGS

DAD BAYLY USED TO SAY, "O LORD, BURN ETERNITY
into my eyeballs." It wasn't original, and it's hard to track down who said it
first. The title of this last section of the book, "last things," points us to the
coming Judgment, Heaven, and Hell. Elders and pastors will be helped by
keeping all three in mind as we do our work.

The Judgment will be held for both the redeemed and the lost. Eternity
burned into our eyeballs here and now will help us become the faithful
servants who will receive the supreme commendation from our Lord, "Well
done, good and faithful slave."[1] We must live in light of these last things.

Jesus often warned His disciples to work hard at being faithful stewards:

Who then is the faithful and sensible slave whom his master put in
charge of his household to give them their food at the proper time?

1. Matthew 25:21, 23.

Blessed is that slave whom his master finds so doing when he comes. Truly I say to you that he will put him in charge of all his possessions. But if that evil slave says in his heart, "My master is not coming for a long time," and begins to beat his fellow slaves and eat and drink with drunkards; the master of that slave will come on a day when he does not expect him and at an hour which he does not know, and will cut him in pieces and assign him a place with the hypocrites; in that place there will be weeping and gnashing of teeth.[2]

God has called us to give His sheep their food at the proper time. This is the work of elders and pastors, but it's hard to live in light of eternity's Heaven and Hell.

"Dichotomous thinking" has become a pejorative term, particularly in relation to sexuality. Dichotomous thinking breaks everything down into black/white, yes/no, true/false, either/or, good/bad. Also, male/female, and that's a no-no today.

The modern conceit is that dichotomy's rigidity gives comfort to the simpleminded and insecure. However, no one separated things into such dichotomies more than Jesus. He spoke of right and wrong, sin and righteousness, the wide and narrow paths, male and female, and Heaven and Hell. Then, throughout His preaching and teaching ministry, He reinforced what He was saying by speaking of blessings and curses. He spoke all the time about Heaven and Hell because He knew it was helpful for us to have eternity burned into our eyeballs.

This is how we'll bring this work on the eldership to an end. First, we'll speak of our accountability before God in light of that great Day of Judgment. Second, we'll speak of the blessings God provides His faithful shepherds, both in this life and in the life to come. These are our "last things."

---

2. Matthew 24:45–51.

It is a sad case, that good men should settle themselves so long in the constant neglect of so great a duty [church discipline]. The common cry is, "Our people are not ready for it; they won't bear it." But is not the fact rather, that you will not bear the trouble and hatred which it will occasion?

—*Richard Baxter,*
The Reformed Pastor

CHAPTER 13

Men Who Must Give an Account

THE INTERNET IS FILLED WITH NEW AND OLD accounts of pastors and elders, as well as boards of trustees, who have failed to address various forms of abuse, and who are now being shamed and fired. We write "failed," not because anyone's been tried and found guilty, but because we find the accounts—particularly the first-person ones—believable. We knew about some of the highest-profile before they became public, but we were not in a position to expose them or discipline those involved. In some of the other cases, there is so much first-hand testimony that we find ourselves saying that, at a minimum, where there's smoke, there's fire.

Yes, some of the cases are a witch hunt and should be shut down, but who shuts down the internet? We're grateful that in a few of the cases we were in a position to expose the sin and to push the authorities who had overlooked it to discipline the leader (although usually those authorities disciplined it against their will).

One of those cases was the refusal of the elders and pastors of one of the highest-profile Presbyterian churches in the country to discipline a

well-known staff member who had engaged in wicked abuse of young men
in his church and from the college where he taught. The church also made
no effort to find and minister to the victims of this man. It took a couple
years of the most strenuous labor on the part of many, including two lawyers
who were elders in our own and another church, to bring the responsible
pastors and session to admit their failure. Sadly, though, their admission
was largely grudging and resentful, and they ended up giving hundreds of
thousands of dollars to the perp to settle his lawsuit, while giving nothing
to his victims.

Why do we bring this up?

Because Scripture is filled with warnings that authorities are accountable
to God for guarding their sheep. We could fill the next several pages with
such warnings, but we'll stick to the single one we have cited repeatedly
in this book:

> Obey your leaders and submit to them, for they keep watch over your
> souls as those who will give an account.[1]

Elders and pastors keep watch over the souls of the sheep; elders and
pastors will give an account for how they used or abused their authority.

Cover-ups and Abuse

As we've pointed out before, "abuse" is the betrayal of authority. The "bad-
use" of authority.

Abuse can take many forms, but the most common one today is not
men using their sheep for their own financial gain, fame, power, or sexual
depravity. The most common today is men in positions of authority refusing to guard their sheep. Refusing to lift a finger to protect their sheep
from the Devil and the wicked men under his sway.

Talking to one of the victims of the tall-steeple Presbyterian church's
staff member, one of us said to him, "You know, I'm not as upset over the
sexually perverted abuse —— perpetrated against you and the others as I

---

1. Hebrews 13:17.

am over the refusal of your pastors and elders to do anything to discipline their staff member and find his victims and minister to them."

Now we know that might sound insensitive to readers who might think this abuse victim would consider that statement insensitive towards the depth of his own and other victims' suffering, but if you could talk to him, you'd find him in full agreement.[2]

The sexually depraved we will always have with us. This is not to excuse sexual perversion nor the abuse of authority in service of that perversion, which leaves sheep wounded for a lifetime, sometimes losing their faith. It is about precisely such wounded sheep that Jesus gives His most sober warning:

> It is inevitable that stumbling blocks come, but woe to him through whom they come! It would be better for him if a millstone were hung around his neck and he were thrown into the sea, than that he would cause one of these little ones to stumble.[3]

It should make us tremble in fear.

But note that Jesus prefaced his warning with a simple statement of fact: "It is inevitable that stumbling blocks come." Sexual perverts, let alone the greedy and narcissists, we will always have with us. Read church history. Read the Bible. Read the story of Lot and King David and the Christians in Corinth.

Now ask yourself which is worse: the wicked man who molests the young; or the elder, pastor, or member of the board of trustees who covers it up?

Yes, we know there may be justifiable reasons why elders and pastors didn't go to the police with the abuser twenty and thirty years ago. We understand how easy it is for the younger today to condemn their fathers in the faith, using best practices of today to condemn what church officers thought was the best pastoral approach yesterday. And by "pastoral," we are not trying to paint cowardice of past church officers in a warm color, as in, "He was just trying to be pastoral." The word "pastoral" should never be

2. This account and the one related below are included with the permission of the victims.
3. Luke 17:1-2.

used as a synonym for fear, weakness, and conniving at wickedness which has the intended effect of avoiding public controversy or holding on to one's job.

We make this point because there are many times when wicked sexual depredations are not taken to the police, despite their being felonies and the accountability to the civil magistrate being clear. This is often because women—mothers and wives—absolutely refuse to allow the police to be told. Sadly, pastors and elders then justify not telling the proper authorities by claiming that they are simply being "pastoral."

One of us worked on bringing a very old sin to accountability by gathering all the principals in our office and mediating a discussion among them of what had actually happened fifteen years earlier. It was eye-opening. In the end, it was clear that both the pastor and the mother of the victim had failed seriously, and the pastors and elders now working with them to address the sins of the distant past had sympathy for both of them.

Here's what had happened:

A leading man in this pastor's church had come to the pastor and confessed his sexual abuse of one of his own stepdaughters. The pastor told him he would be at his house first thing the next morning to take him down to the police station to confess his crimes.

When the pastor arrived at the man's home to pick him up, the mother of the victim forbade her husband to leave the house and pleaded with her pastor not to tell anyone about her husband's crimes. In this she was typical of mothers of abused children. She didn't want her daughter to have to go through interrogation and court testimony. She didn't want the incest in her home to become public. She was petrified and made it clear that only the most abusive pastor would put a woman and her daughter from his church through such terrible suffering.

He was a young pastor—young and inexperienced. No one at his seminary had ever talked to him about such situations. He was in over his head, and he acceded to the mother's demands.

But now, fifteen years later, another of this same woman's daughters was sitting in front of us with her mother, her new husband, her former pastor, and several of her present pastors, telling this former pastor and her own mother that the consequence of not going to the police was that she herself continued to be abused. For years.

We could recount a number of other situations similar to this, but everyone knows such stories, and we've all learned to act as if we would have done the right thing ten, twenty, or thirty years ago. If we were honest with ourselves, we would know it's arguable, at best.

Since this penultimate chapter is titled, "Men Who Must Give an Account," it's clear we do not excuse this pastor—and we didn't. He left the meeting in terrible grief, and we think he's likely never recovered from it. We're happy to report that the victim in that office with us that evening has recovered and is now a very happy wife and mother.

Her mother also left that meeting in terrible grief. Before the meeting was over, both she and her former pastor were clearly made to see how they had sinned against the victims, and they did not defend themselves (which, of course, was very healing for the victim). When elders and pastors bring wickedness to the bar of God's justice in the church and before the civil magistrate, it's both terribly painful and wonderfully healing. So do the hard thing, because the hard thing is usually the right thing.

Things like birth and death and war and sex clarify matters. Incest and child abuse and rape are still against the law, and it is the duty of elders and pastors to report these crimes, or to immediately escort the criminal to the civil magistrate to confess his crimes himself. Submit yourselves and your sheep to the civil magistrate because he is appointed by God to punish evil.

Sin in Our Midst

But what if your fellow elder or pastor is the sinner? What if your pastor is stealing money from the church? What if your youth pastor is raping the minor boys or girls in his youth group? What if another elder is committing adultery? What if the pastor is preaching grace without repentance? What if one of the elders confesses he abused his elementary school cousin thirty years ago when he was in high school? What if the pastor tells you—confidentially, of course—that he thinks he's come to believe in women elders? What if the lead pastor's wife is a gossip? What if it's commonly known that another elder's son is living with a man?—*Living* with a man, if you get our meaning. What if the associate pastor's daughter tells the kids at school that she's a lesbian? What if you go to the presbytery meeting and the men present approve a man's ordination who thinks it's fine to starve someone to death if their quality of life isn't the best and they want to die? What if one of the church's Sunday school teachers is telling the children in her class that Mormons are Christians too? What if your denominational seminary supports its students who come out as gay and intend to serve in the denomination as youth pastors and campus-ministry workers? What if your pastor preaches grace without repentance?—Yes, this is an intentional repetition. What if your pastor is an antinomian, but none of the other elders know what "antinomian" is, let alone that it destroys the very souls for whom Christ died?

Reading through the list above, some readers might think to themselves, *What kind of churches do these men serve? Is their congregation the inmates of some state correctional facility? Thank goodness our church isn't like that! Incest? Murder? Rape? Mormons are Christians? Grace without repentance? No, not in my church.*

We could respond in a number of ways, but just a couple before we end.

First of all, keep in mind we are two entirely different pastors ministering in two entirely different contexts nationally, educationally, ecclesiastically, linguistically, and culturally. The homeland of one of us is the United States of America, and the homeland of the other is Germany. One of us has an MDiv from a Boston seminary, and the other has a PhD from the University of Bonn. One of us was ordained in the Presbyterian Church (USA), where he held membership for ten years, then brought his congregation into the Presbyterian Church in America, where he served for another twenty; the other has been a member and currently serves as a pastor in Germany's non-state Free Evangelical Church. One of us ministers to a congregation comprised largely of North Americans with a small group of international students, mostly from China; the other ministers to a congregation made up of about half native Germans and half North Africans, many of whom arrived in Germany as refugees. Both of our congregations have a sermon in English and a sermon in a different language each Lord's Day. We will dispense with summaries of our two differing cultures.

We've described the significant differences in our ministry contexts to make the point that neither of us would write the above list any differently. We're both aware of all these sins within the church, and many more equally as serious. We both testify that these things are characteristic of the world we live in, and therefore the churches we serve. But really, these things have always been characteristic of the churches elders and pastors serve.

One encouraging thing you can do is buy a copy of the consistory (session) minutes of Calvin and his fellow pastors and elders of the church of Geneva five centuries ago, which we quoted from in chapter 8. These are fascinating records of the work Calvin and his fellow pastors and elders of Geneva did each week on Thursdays. Here they summarize their pastoral approach in correcting sins they called "crimes"—sinful behavior which included "negligen[ce] in coming to church" and "secret vices":

> When there are crimes that do not merit only remonstrances in words, but corrections with punishment, if anyone has fallen into these, according to the needs of the case it will be necessary to order him to abstain for some time from Communion to humble himself before God and better recognize his fault . . .
>
> And nevertheless let all this be so measured that there is no rigor by which anyone will be grieved and so that the corrections will be merely medicines to bring back sinners to Our Lord.[4]

It was hard work each Thursday as they met, and Calvin was not without other hard work occupying his time. Several estimates place the number of adults (communicants) in Geneva summoned before this consistory each year at one in fifteen, or six to seven percent of the adult population.[5] Imagine the time this consumed with the pastors, elders, and Calvin himself!

We must get to know our sheep and love them enough to do this work today.

Now then, our dear brothers, we have work to do. It's hard work we won't ever do unless we are reminded that we will soon give an account to Almighty God for our protection of His rams, ewes, and lambs. Stop and consider that, dear brothers; stop and consider that.

---

4. Kingdon, 420–21.
5. Ibid., xviii, n2.

Therefore, since we have so great a cloud of witnesses surrounding us, let us also lay aside every encumbrance and the sin which so easily entangles us, and let us run with endurance the race that is set before us, fixing our eyes on Jesus, the author and perfecter of faith, who for the joy set before Him endured the cross, despising the shame, and has sat down at the right hand of the throne of God.

For consider Him who has endured such hostility by sinners against Himself, so that you will not grow weary and lose heart.

—Hebrews 12:1–3

CHAPTER 14

The Joy Set before Us

ARE YOU SEEING THAT GREAT CLOUD OF witnesses? Do you hear them cheering on God's faithful servants? Jesus is the Author and Finisher of our faith, and He Himself, God Almighty, endured the cross and despised its shame. He Himself endured the terrible hostility of sinners.

We must not grow weary and lose heart. Our suffering is less and our crosses smaller than His.

But we are tempted, aren't we? No doubt some of us fantasize about resigning our office. The work is hard and often thankless—particularly if we're looking to the sheep for our reward.

What was it that kept Jesus faithful?

Many things, but here we are explicitly told that Jesus was helped to endure the cross and despise its shame by anticipating "the joy set before Him" (v. 2).

Back when Mary Lee and I first entered the pastorate, we were invited to dinner with a young couple who were about to leave for a new life as missionaries in Africa. We heard the story of their call to mission work in its entirety. They told us how they had wrestled over the decision, particularly in light of having to give up their family farm handed down through the generations. They had been working that farm, but now they were about to leave it behind, with no plans to return. It had been weighing heavily on them—leaving friends and family behind, but particularly leaving the family farm.

Then they told how they had been reading in the Gospel of Mark. "Listen to this," they said with great excitement, proceeding to read these words:

> Peter began to say to Him, "Behold, we have left everything and followed You." Jesus said, "Truly I say to you, there is no one who has left house or brothers or sisters or mother or father or children or farms, for My sake and for the gospel's sake, but that he will receive a hundred times as much now in the present age, houses and brothers and sisters and mothers and children and farms, along with persecutions; and in the age to come, eternal life."[1]

"We couldn't believe it! It says 'farms'!"

The evening was joyful because our hosts were joyful—in anticipation of the joy set before them by the Word of God.

We don't mean to make light of the difficulties of the eldership. There's good reason the Apostle Peter exhorts elders:

> Therefore, I exhort the elders among you, as your fellow elder and witness of the sufferings of Christ, and a partaker also of the glory that is to be revealed, shepherd the flock of God among you, exercising oversight not under compulsion, but voluntarily, according to the will of God; and not for sordid gain, but with eagerness; nor yet as lording it over those allotted to your charge, but proving to be examples to the flock.

Peter immediately follows these sober words with a marvelous promise: "And when the Chief Shepherd appears, you will receive the unfading crown of glory."[2]

1. Mark 10:28–30.
2. 1 Peter 5:1–4.

Such promises are all through Scripture:

As it is written, Eye hath not seen, nor ear heard, neither have entered into the heart of man, the things which God hath prepared for them that love him.[3]

If Jesus lived for the joy set before Him, it's no failure on our part to think on these things and motivate ourselves by all these wonderful promises.

But also, let me give a small testimony Jürgen agrees with wholeheartedly.

First of all, you should know that one of the ways I explain how much I love my wife, Mary Lee, is by telling other pastors that I've never ever had her put pressure on me to compromise my work for the sake of our family's stability, security, or financial well-being. Never once. The same is true for Jürgen's wife, Ilse.

When I say this, other (usually younger) pastors give me a knowing look, and sometimes envy me. The dangers, toils, and snares of pastors are particularly sneaky and constant, so we often have occasion to fantasize about another day job. Of course, that's not what the pastor is called to, and he can't simply resign his office and go cut grass—much as he might want to.

But shame on me, because the fact that Mary Lee has never put the slightest pressure on me to be unfaithful for the sake of our family does not mean I haven't been unfaithful. I testify to it publicly that there are countless times I have left undone what I should have done and done what is forbidden. I am a sinner; but not just any sinner, I am a sinner-pastor.

I make that confession so that readers will not see my temptations and failures as categorically different from theirs, nor my achievements as superior to theirs.

Now then, my testimony—one which I have often given to pastors:

Never once, when I have had the faith to die for the sake of the name of Jesus and the authority of His Word and the protection and well-being of His sheep, has He failed to give me (along with persecutions, yes) a hundred times now in the present age whatever piddling, trifling thing I

3. 1 Corinthians 2:9 (KJV).

had mourned over giving up. When, by faith, I have been enabled to lay in dust life's glory dead, without fail there has blossomed red from the ground life that shall endless be.[4]

Yes, you are weak, as are we. Yes, you are a sinner, as are we. Yes, you are foolish, as are we. Yes, you are faithless, as are we.

But with God, all things are possible.

Look at the joy set before you, both in the present age, and in the age to come. Savor that promise given directly to you, an elder: "When the Chief Shepherd appears, you will receive the unfading crown of glory."

Both of us are near the end of our ministries. Neither of our congregations are anything to brag about in worldly terms. But in view of Heaven and eternity, both of us hit our foreheads and ask ourselves if we're living a dream or if this is reality, that we have such love and joy in our marriages and families—but particularly in our congregations. Such intimacy. Such love. Such wonderful elders we have worked with. Such godly men and women, boys and girls, helping us preach each Lord's Day.

Dad Bayly always used to remind me, "God is no man's debtor."

That He isn't. He repays us one hundred times in this age, and in the age to come.

Sure, "with persecutions." But can we not echo the joy of those first church officers in Jerusalem who, after being "flogged" by the Sanhedrin, responded by "rejoicing that they had been considered worthy to suffer shame for His name"?

You got that, right? *Rejoicing.*

Then Scripture adds this sweet note: "And every day, in the temple and from house to house, they kept right on teaching and preaching Jesus as the Christ."[5]

They went back to work shepherding the sheep.

This reminds us of the shepherds keeping watch over their flocks by night to whom God's angels revealed the birth of Jesus. After they had come in haste and found Mary, Joseph, and the Babe wrapped in swaddling clothes, lying in a manger, we are told, "the shepherds returned, glorifying and praising God."[6]

---

4. George Matheson, "O Love That Will Not Let Me Go," st. 4.
5. Acts 5:40–42
6. Luke 2:12, 16, 20 (KJV).

"Returned"? To what?

They returned to guarding their sheep.

Now then, two things five centuries old from our dear brother, Pastor Martin Bucer. First an exhortation, and then a prayer.

The exhortation:

When St Peter is asked for the third time if he loves the Lord, and himself for the third time protests his love, then for the third time the Lord says to him: "Feed my sheep." It is as if he were saying: If you love me so much and want to show this by your actions, feed my sheep, because there is nothing you can do for me which is preferable or more pleasing to me.

If we really love Christ, he is everything to us; therefore if anyone is called to this ministry, whatever unpleasantness, sufferings and crosses he may have to bear in the course of his ministry, he will be upheld and strengthened against all unpleasantness, sufferings and crosses only by the fact that the Lord Jesus has commanded him to do this, and commanded it as the highest ministry of love that we can show him. Then each one will feel as Paul did when he writes about himself in 1 Corinthians 9: "Yet when I preach the gospel, I cannot boast, for I am compelled to preach. Woe to me if I do not preach the gospel! If I preach voluntarily, I have a reward; if not voluntarily, I am simply discharging the trust committed to me."[7]

"I am simply discharging the trust committed to me," says the dear apostle; for that should be more than enough for any Christian, if he is called to this ministry, to accept it and carry it out with all faithfulness, withstanding and suffering whatever trouble, labour, abuse, shame, suffering and cross he may meet in the course of it. . . .

. . . There is so much delightful consolation for us in the fact that in this way we are showing the greatest love to our Lord Jesus, by serving him in his dear church which he has purchased with his precious blood, which is his dear spouse and his body.

And we end with his prayer:

---

7. 1 Corinthians 9:16–17.

May the Lord Jesus, our chief Shepherd and Bishop, grant us such elders and carers of souls as will seek his lambs which are still lost, bring back those which have wandered, heal those which are wounded, strengthen those which are sickly, and guard and feed in the right way those which are healthy, in the way we have described. Those who are sheep and not goats will allow themselves to be brought by such carers of souls and ministers of Christ through the word of the Lord into Christ's church and into his sheep-fold, and to be kept in it, healed, strengthened, guarded and fed, in all things obeying and gladly following him. For anyone who is born of God hears his word, and Christ's sheep hear his word and follow him.[8]

May God bless you in your work, our dear fellow elders.

8. Bucer, 192–93.

Scripture Index

THANK YOU
to everyone who supports
OUT OF OUR MINDS through Patreon,
with special thanks to the following patrons:

Cody Carnett
Jim & Annie Hogue
Matthew & Sarah Hoover
Matthieu LaCroix
Andreas Mack
Karl Russo
Adam Spaetti
Jeffrey Sparks

To support the writing ministry of Tim Bayly,
including future projects like this one, go
to **patreon.com/outofourminds**

CPSIA information can be obtained
at www.ICGtesting.com
Printed in the USA
LVHW051708280820
664259LV00005B/121